OUVERT

9 HEURES

BREAKFAST LUNCH TEA

BY
ROSE CARRARINI

BREAKFAST
LUNCH
TEA

ROSE BAKERY

CONTENTS

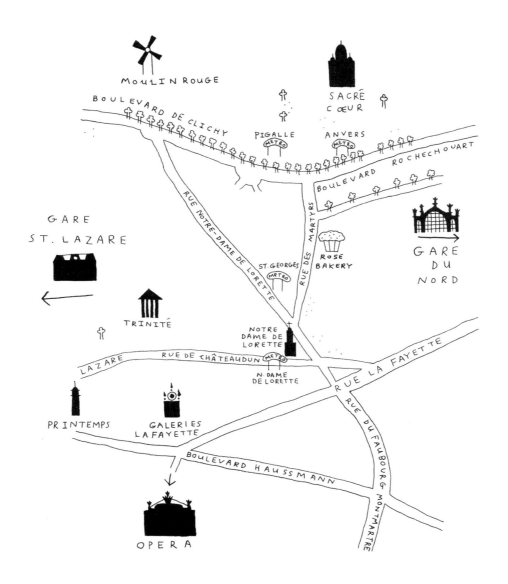

ROSE BAKERY
46, RUE DES MARTYRS
75009 PARIS
01 42 82 12 80

INTRODUCTION

ALL ABOUT ME

I am not a trained chef. Everything I have achieved has been a result of learning from other chefs, responding to customers' desires, reading lots and, most of all, knowing so strongly what I want from foods... their intrinsic health benefits, their taste and look, and ultimately, my choice of some foods and rejection of others. I have always been extremely picky, selecting this tomato and not that one, this well-reared chicken and not the other, and so on.

I am not very fond of sweet things and sugar, and yet I became a pastry chef. I couldn't find the pastries and desserts that I wanted anywhere, and neither could the customers of Villandry, the small «épicerie fine» in London that we created in 1988. One day, I decided to make quiches to add to Villandry's display of sandwiches. I searched for a good basic recipe for shortcrust pastry, «pâte brisée», compared notes and discovered that the recipes were simple and more or less very similar. So, with the first trials a huge success, this basic recipe was the beginning of my work with pastry.

«How do you make your pastry?» was a common question at the time. «Just like everyone else,» I replied. All the same, I knew from the positive reaction I was getting that something important was happening, and so I began a painstaking study of sweet and savoury baking. Inspiration came from many sources, including the wonderful Alice Waters and her restaurant Chez Panisse in Berkeley, California, as well as writers such as Richard Olney and Elizabeth David, for their simplicity and their ability to capture the essence of what food should be about. I soon found that following recipes was not enough – the way you handle dough, the right moment to take a cake out of the oven, the touch and smell of things, these are just as important. Even the way you work in different weather conditions can affect recipes enormously. Choosing the right ingredients is equally vital – the ingredients you choose should make you feel good, whether they are organic or not, wholemeal or white, milk or non-dairy, and so on. I spent the first ten years of my life in South Africa, and have been searching ever since for the intense flavours that I experienced there. I am constantly trying to create ways of bringing back that intensity in my recipes, so it made sense for me to be strict about trying to use only ingredients that are in season.

A CHANGE OF DIRECTION

Only a few years before establishing Villandry, my husband Jean-Charles and I were still running a knitwear business, travelling regularly to Italy, France and Japan for work. But it became increasingly obvious that our real interests

ROSE CARRARINI

lay elsewhere: instead of rushing to the fashion stores, we would seek out the local food markets, the best sources of bread and the particularly special restaurants.

I think it is fair to say that a single experience can inspire you in a major way and then go on to guide your work. For us this changing point came when we ate at the Hyakumizon restaurant in Tokyo, run by Fukiko Yokoyama. She was reinventing traditional Japanese cuisine using vegetables as her base. I will never forget the simple dishes of vegetables, which were cut in special ways, and the intense flavours she created. One particular bowl was just carrot. No sauce. No garnish. No fuss. No flourish. Food must not look contrived or stiff or artificial. It should have its own dynamic, looking natural, and right. The taste was intense and exquisite, and was mostly of the carrot itself. Possibly blanched, cooled, cooked again in a dashi and flashed under a grill, this dish was one of the most humble yet delicious dishes we have ever had the privilege of tasting. Whatever the techniques she had used, I was convinced that you don't need any fuss or flourish, as it's the flavour of the dish that counts.

At this time, we always came home to London laden with local food specialities that we had bought on our travels. We were frustrated shoppers, with most of our favourite groceries only found abroad. London was not the place it is now, full of thriving farmers' markets, delicatessens and wonderful restaurants. I remember dashing around town twenty years ago, searching for organic vegetables. Now of course they are available everywhere and that is wonderful. Back then, we saw a hole in the market that we could fill, or at least begin to fill. At the end of 1986, we finally decided to close our knitwear business and took a year out to research and find a location for our own food store. We travelled to food fairs in France and Italy and were amazed at what we saw, at the same time learning very quickly to distinguish between beautiful packaging and top-quality food. After sourcing all the products we wanted, we opened Villandry early in 1988. Its concept, if that is what you can call it, was unlike any other place at the time. What we really wanted to do was to bring a whole market into one tiny space and I think we almost achieved it.

Thankfully, the process of my becoming a chef or cook was a gradual one. Villandry began by selling sandwiches, soup and of course quiches, but pastries and cakes soon followed. Finally we acquired the space to open a seated area where we could serve proper meals, which we were able to do thanks to the generous help of wonderful Irish chefs from Ballymaloe in County Cork. Their guidance in

OUR BUTCHER, GERARD FOLLIOT (RIGHT)
WITH RAYMOND PAILLEAU

those early days was inspirational and set me on the right road. Villandry was a very complicated business, which required superhuman efforts to keep on the right track, to keep it a true, honest and wholesome place. So Rose Bakery, the shop and restaurant we opened in Paris in 2002, is the culmination of years of our removing what is not necessary, of keeping the simple, good things and of changing with the times. I never wanted to serve fussy or complex food – my intention was always to dissolve the distinction between home and restaurant cooking. Rose Bakery feels right for today, a place of feeling and familiarity, serving food that is close to my heart.

ROSE BAKERY

So at long last there was a place where I could fully express my ideas, ideas distilled from the previous 15 years of experiences. Yet Rose Bakery is simple and natural, and most definitely a grand step away from traditional restaurant concepts. There was always great joy at the table in our home, with simplicity and freshness in the food that we prepared, and yet the food at restaurants often seemed contrived and disappointing to me, straining to be different. So at Rose Bakery we try to prepare, cook and eat everything fresh on the same day. It is extremely lucky that most things sell out, so we rarely have to wonder how to preserve food for another day!

Jean-Charles discovered an old «chartil» (a place where the old fruit barrows for the markets were kept) near the Gare du Nord. It hadn't been used for years and was terribly dark and decrepit. But this is the kind of space that inspires Jean-Charles, and so within six months of his finding it, Rose Bakery was born, without a traditional shop window, and with only the wonderful door to entice you in. We have always felt that food doesn't need a big design to show it off, so we kept away from trendy materials and kept the concrete that was already there. The tables were made from concrete and metal by a friend, the simple white counters held up by garden stands. The back wall was painted by an artist friend, Lindy, who rushed in with her paints the day before we opened and finished our space with a lovely wall of colour. Our packaging was plain and white, free of design and marketing. The only objects that we chose very carefully were the wonderful hand-thrown plates, bowls and cups, which we had made by the potters at a cooperative called Made in Cley, located in the village of Cley next the Sea in Norfolk, England. Our cutlery was made by David Mellor in Sheffield, in the north of England.

In Rose Bakery, the boundaries between shop window, counter, dining area and kitchens are blurred. The display on the counter is also the window display, capturing the eyes

JEAN-LUC POUJAURAN,
WHO SUPPLIES OUR BREAD

of both the passers-by and the lunch clientèle. The dining area and retail section are sandwiched between the two kitchens, so there is a constant sense of theatre, with trays of food continuously on the move and customers peering over to check what everything is, with lots of «oohs» and «aahs»! Such displays of freshness, tastes and textures have created a place where customers instantly relax and give us their trust.

We wanted to create a place where people felt at home, somewhere that they came back to often, where the design was timeless and the quality of the food shone. We wanted a place where creativity was possible, with total harmony amongst its staff (you need lots of smiles and kindness when the work can be hard and relentless). And above all, we wanted to create a restaurant that ranked vegetables above meat or fish. When we opened Rose Bakery, it was a lovely surprise to find many similar-minded people; customers who were drawn to raw salads and fresh and simple cooking. There are some who prefer not to mix protein and starches, and others who can't eat wheat or other ingredients; there are chefs who might find this irritating, but it inspires me and I plan all our menus with such different needs in mind.

FOOD SOURCES

Having arrived in Paris from London quite suddenly and then having found the site for Rose Bakery much more quickly than expected, our excitement with the project was such that food sourcing lost out at first. We had always worked with good and trustworthy suppliers in London but, in Paris, we knew no one. We were advised to find a «maraîcher» or market gardener at our local market and to persuade them to supply us. This proved difficult as there was no accessible market near us, a really good one in Montrouge couldn't deliver, and we had no time to drive around Paris. Eventually, a customer who lived nearby recommended her local organic shop as a possible supplier. Thank goodness that Sebastien, the owner, agreed, as he proved to be our lifeline, understanding what we wanted, delivering all our vegetables and some of the fruit, chicken and milk. After a while he put us in touch with his source at Rungis, the large wholesale market in Paris, and now we are beginning to source some produce from farms not too far from the city.

One supplier, Earl Baubion from the Eure-et-Loir region, brings us his wonderful onions and potatoes. Our butcher, Gerard Folliot, who has been working in the rue Sainte Anne for 20 years, sources his meat carefully from selected farms and chooses only the very best. Even if the meat is

DAVID, LINDA AND BEN DEME
AT CHEGWORTH VALLEY FARM,
WHO SUPPLY OUR APPLES

not always organic, it is well-reared and completely traceable to its source. Our organic smoked salmon comes from Ireland via a French importer. In season, we import English apples (Cox's, Bramleys, Russets, etc.) from Chegworth Valley Farm in Kent as I'm afraid French apples cannot compete. For almost 15 years, we have known Jean-Luc Poujauran, who makes some of the best bread in France and gave me lots of advice before we opened Rose Bakery. We had been begging him to supply us for a long time, but we were never in his area for deliveries. Finally, in 2006, he agreed. We are truly happy and so are our customers.

Our teas come from a tea broker in Suffolk and Jardins de Gaïa in France but there was never any doubt as to where our coffee was coming from – Union Coffee Roasters in east London. Their wonderful roasts and Fairtrade ethics convinced us, and the coffee is so good that it is selling even better than we expected. Our cheeses come from Neal's Yard in London, with whom we have been working for years. We were very careful not to import too many British cheeses at first as our French customers still favour local cheeses, but Cheddar and Stilton are already very well known in France, and always sell well. We are slowly introducing others, such as Caerphilly, Spenwood and two of my favourites, Wensleydale and Berkswell. Our aim, as always, is to find more local growers and suppliers.

We try to use organic produce as much as possible, but this cannot always be achieved, especially in our baking (see page 31 for notes on ingredients and cooking tips). First and foremost we have always tried to find what's the best ingredient for a recipe, be it organic or just the right quality of product. The final choice is a personal decision you have to make and be happy with. What I will say is that for about 30 years I have preferred to eat organic where possible, mainly as I feel that eating fewer chemicals is better for you. As consumers, we have very little choice as to how or where things are grown and reared so I choose organic, as I feel that this must be better for health. I am not talking about comparative flavours, nutrients and all the other arguments here. Just simply that organic makes me feel better.

However, it will always be infinitely better to eat a crisp, locally grown lettuce than a limp organic one. Choosing food that is sourced locally is equally if not more important than whether it is organic or not. I feel good about the locally grown food that a few «maraîchers» sell at some markets in Paris, as they use hardly any pesticides and fertilizers. I trust them. Their produce is also incredibly fresh, having been just picked that morning. So the choice is down to a question of trust and being lucky enough to have those choices. Choice is everything.

CHEESE FROM NEAL'S YARD IN LONDON

THE VEGETABLE DELIVERY

VEGETABLES READY FOR SALE

DIALOGUE

We have always enjoyed an open and valuable dialogue with our customers. The smell and sight of our counters brings in passers-by, and we have found that people know what will taste good when they see it. Observing such reactions and holding long conversations with our customers (some of whom have become lasting friends) are key to our outlook and success. Jean-Charles is truly the face of Rose Bakery, dealing with our customers and suppliers on a daily basis. In fact, when he goes around Paris now, he is greeted everywhere as «Monsieur Bakery»!

Every place that Jean-Charles and I have created has begun quite modestly. Strengthened by customer support, we have grown in location and ideas, evolving continually. When Rei Kawakubo asked if I would consider taking the space on the top floor of Dover Street Market, the store she set up in London in 2005, I did not hesitate. The concept was to create a very simple version of the Parisian Rose Bakery, serving light and healthy meals as well as cakes. We sat together for about an hour designing it (we both work fast, and understood each other immediately) and within a matter of weeks, the units were made and shipped to London from Japan – an extraordinary achievement. The place in London is at once calm and fun, and works well. We are so happy with it that we are now searching for new sites in Paris...

Despite the changes over the years, we have kept to our principal aims: to maintain a high quality in what we do and produce; to increase the use of organic ingredients; to introduce more vegetable-based dishes; and to offer (if possible) healthier desserts and cakes, without compromising flavour and texture. We are also developing a gluten and dairy-free range. Before Rose Bakery, our premises were half «épicerie» and half restaurant/take-out. We now produce 90 per cent of the food and products we sell, as our own homemade food always sold best and made customers feel that they had discovered something special.

Many of the happiest moments of my life have been spent round a table, eating. With Rose Bakery we wanted to create a place that was happy, even when temperatures were rising, it was too full and we didn't have enough hands to cope with the rush. There are times when I believe we have achieved this. Often, when you are exhausted and wonder where you will find the energy to continue, a customer will say something like, «We have been coming here so often and for so long because we just love the food. It feels like someone is cooking especially for us, and it is exactly the kind of food we like, food that it is impossible to find elsewhere.» At this point, my mind clouds over with emotion and I don't know what to reply. That complete understanding is wonderful, and we all just end up thanking each other.

IN THE 9TH ARRONDISSEMENT

OUR MAIN ENTRANCE

THE RESTAURANT

THE PINK FRIDGE

THE COUNTER

TECHNIQUES & INGREDIENTS

PLANNING THE MENU

SOME TECHNIQUES TO REMEMBER

I work, like many other cooks, instinctively. You just can't predict how waterlogged some fruits are going to be, or how tough this meat is or how delicate that fish is, or whether a particular beetroot will roast in one or three hours. You can have an idea when you start off, but nothing is ever the same twice, especially in baking. When I read recipes from other cookbooks, I simply look at the ingredients and proceed with them in my own way. But when I ask someone else to do that, the results are often different from mine. So in this book I have written the recipes exactly as I explain them to people working with me at Rose Bakery, as the instructions are so important, almost more important than the ingredients. For instance, pastry has to be handled in special ways, but if you add an extra handful of flour to the recipe, or less butter, it won't matter too much. You can substitute pears or plums in an apple crumble, or brown sugar for white, and so on. The instructions are especially important when you are baking – when you are cooking or making salads, the dishes will still work if you make changes or even if you get things wrong. You can change an ingredient but you cannot really change a technique successfully.

It is very important that you feel free to add different ingredients or change things as you go along. Our recipes are made with that in mind. It is so much to do with instinct, and measuring can only give you an approximate idea. For instance a cup measure can vary enormously. We use a light scoop method, but you may fill your cup more than we do. A lemon can vary in size and render very different quantities of juice, a shallot is small and gentle in flavour but its far bigger sister, the onion, has a stronger flavour to correspond to its size. You may prefer a sweeter cake, so you can add more sugar, and so on. That is what cooking is all about. At Rose Bakery we try to use as near to the same measurements each time as possible, but the cake or cookies or soup or whatever will inevitably turn out slightly differently every time. That is the mystery and the fun of cooking.

MOISTURE
Add more liquid or more dry ingredients when the recipe does not seem to be working for you... a sticky dough is not right, and neither is a dry and crumbly one. Dough must always feel right and be easy to work with.

OVEN TEMPERATURES
Oven temperatures vary, so do use your own judgment and knowledge of your oven. The best thing to do is check your dish a good 10–15 minutes before my times, as I have only given approximate timings.

PEELING OR NOT
Sometimes we peel fruit and vegetables, and sometimes we don't. Often we half-peel fruit, alternating stripes of peel and flesh. The choice is yours.

CHOOSING INGREDIENTS

There are several important points to note about the kinds of food I use and the way I use them. As our recipes are mostly very simple, the secret to getting a wonderful result lies ultimately in the ingredients. So choose them well. Wherever possible the ingredients I use are organic. This applies to fruit, vegetables, dairy products, meats and fish, as well as to eggs, flours and sugars. At Rose Bakery, however, we do not use organic butter as I have found it to contain too much water. Not all the sugars we use are organic either, as I have found organic light brown sugar to be too hard, and other types of sugar not quite fine enough. We also haven't found a good organic cream... yet.

BUTTER
We always use unsalted butter in our baking recipes. I like to use a French butter called Lescure, as I have found it to have the lowest water content, which helps to make the lightest pastry.

CHOCOLATE
The chocolate we use is Valrhona's Guanaja 70 per cent. But Green & Black's Dark or Montezuma's Very Dark 73 per cent are very good, too.

KOHLRABI

Known as «chou rave» in France, this vegetable can be quite difficult to find. Also known as a cabbage turnip, it is a member of the cabbage family and is either pale green or purple in colour. Eaten raw or cooked, it tastes like a turnip or radish. If you can't find kohlrabi, substitute it with turnips or white radishes, such as daikon.

MARIGOLD

We use this brand of bouillon powder as it is delicious and completely monosodium glutamate free, and made from entirely natural ingredients. If you don't have time to make a stock, this is what to use instead. Marigold can be found in most wholefood stores and some supermarkets.

OLIVE OIL

When olive oil is mentioned, I always mean an extra virgin olive oil.

QUINOA

This grain comes from South America and is very digestible, nutty in flavour and rich in vitamins, minerals and protein. Cook it for about 15 minutes as you would rice.

RICE

For risotto, I always use an organic carnaroli rice. But any other risotto rice, such as arborio, will do.

SHOYU

This is a light soy sauce.

VANILLA

We use a natural vanilla extract that is very intense, so we only need to add a drop to our recipes. With a commercial vanilla flavouring (natural or otherwise), you can use up to a teaspoon, as it is much less concentrated.

BREAKFAST

FRUIT

FRESH MIXED FRUIT SALAD
MELON AND GINGER SALAD
COMPÔTE OF APRICOTS AND VANILLA
RHUBARB AND ORANGE
CRÈME ANGLAISE
POACHED PEACHES AND RED FRUITS
FRUIT TABOULÉ

JUICES AND SMOOTHIES

CLASSIC BANANA SMOOTHIE
LIME, GRAPEFRUIT AND GINGER JUICE
TOMATO, CELERY AND SPRING ONION JUICE

CEREALS

SUGAR-FREE GRANOLA
HONEY GRANOLA
RAW MUESLI
TRADITIONAL PORRIDGE

EGGS

PERFECT SCRAMBLED EGGS

PANCAKES

CLASSIC PANCAKES
RICOTTA PANCAKES
GLUTEN-FREE BUCKWHEAT PANCAKES
VEGAN PANCAKES

SCONES

PLAIN SCONES
SULTANA SCONES
BLUEBERRY SCONES
MAPLE SYRUP SCONES
DATE SCONES
CHEDDAR CORNMEAL SCONES

ŒUF À LA COQUE AVEC 'TOAST MARMITE'

BREAKFAST

For most of us, breakfast does not play a big enough part in our busy and rushed lives – if it happens at all. Too often it is a hurried cup of tea or coffee and a slice of toast. So far as we are concerned, breakfast is our favourite meal. One to be lingered over and enjoyed, full of fresh and nourishing foods. And for us the ideal situation for this is one where time is not important, such as weekends, and we can happily cook and prepare a breakfast. Of course, on most mornings toast will do very nicely. However, with these very simple recipes breakfasts get to be a little special, as they should be.

FRUIT

For me, breakfast must always begin with fruit. I love fruit – raw, baked, poached, squeezed…whichever. At Rose Bakery we always try to have two fruit salads a day, one raw and one cooked. Our customers are delighted as so few food places take the time to make fruit salads; they are probably among our most popular desserts and take-outs. Even in winter, when there are really only apples and pears, pears and apples, we try to make fruit salads. They are wonderful whether they are made with only two fruits – grapefruit and apples, apricots and blueberries – or with many. And the choices are endless: seasonal fruits, exotic fruits, dried fruits. In the end you will choose a combination of your favourites. Some pairings don't work, such as apricots and bananas, mangoes and pears, plums and pineapples; and anything with oranges which work only by themselves (or as a zest with rhubarb). The most important thing to remember is to keep the salad moist with just enough juice and sugar. A bowlful of strawberries is really nice, but adding a hint of lemon and even half a teaspoon of sugar can make it great. It's a matter of taking care of the seasoning, as you do with a vegetable salad, and understanding the nature of each fruit.

HALF-PEELED PEARS

FRESH MIXED FRUIT SALAD

Serves 6
1 pineapple
2 red apples
2 kiwi fruit
2 large handfuls strawberries
3 white peaches
2 pink grapefruit
1 lemon
2 tablespoons caster (superfine) **sugar (optional)**
2 large handfuls raspberries or blackberries

Peel the pineapple and remove the 'eyes' from the flesh with a small pointed knife. Cut in half downwards and remove the inner hard core. Slice thinly, then put in a bowl.

Core the apples and cut them into quarters, then into chunky pieces.

Peel and slice the kiwi fruit.

Depending on size, leave the strawberries whole or slice them in half. I like to do both.

Cut each peach into eight wedges.

Put the apples, kiwi fruit, strawberries and peaches into the bowl with the pineapple.

Remove all the skin and pith from the grapefruit and cut the segments into the bowl, squeezing out any extra juice as you go.

Squeeze the lemon over the fruit, and sprinkle with the sugar if you wish.

Mix well and scatter the raspberries or blackberries over the top.

Chill or eat at room temperature within 2 hours. I don't like my fruit too chilled, except for watermelon, as I feel the flavours disappear!

MELON AND GINGER SALAD

Serves 4–5
100 g (½ cup) **caster** (superfine) **sugar**
4 cm (1½ inch) **piece of fresh ginger, finely sliced**
juice of 1 lemon, plus extra to taste
1 orange-fleshed melon, peeled and deseeded
1 green-fleshed melon, peeled and deseeded
a large wedge of watermelon

Put the sugar in a saucepan with 250 ml (1 cup) water and bring to the boil over a gentle heat, stirring constantly until the sugar dissolves.

Add the ginger and leave to cool while the ginger infuses.

Strain the syrup and add the lemon juice.

Cut the melons into chunky pieces and put them in a bowl.

Pour over the syrup and mix well. If the salad tastes too sweet add more lemon juice.

Chill for about 30 minutes.

Variations
I also love:
* Bananas, strawberries and natural (plain) yogurt – a sort of chunky smoothie
* Apples and shredded dates with a pinch of cinnamon
* All the red fruits in any combination
* Mango – with lime juice or just on its own!
* Mixed citrus fruits cut into segments, with a taste of maple syrup

FRESH MIXED FRUIT SALAD

COMPÔTE OF APRICOTS AND VANILLA

Apricots are my favourite fruit but unfortunately today they are rarely as luscious as they are supposed to be. To get them anywhere near that, we poach them gently in a sugar syrup infused with vanilla.

Serves 4
100 g (½ cup) caster (superfine) sugar
1 teaspoon lemon juice
1 vanilla bean, halved lengthways to scatter the seeds
12 apricots, halved and stoned
1 or 2 handfuls blueberries (optional)

Put the sugar in a saucepan with 250 ml (1 cup) water and the lemon juice and vanilla bean, and bring to a gentle simmer, stirring constantly until the sugar dissolves.

Add the apricot halves and poach them until they begin to deepen in colour and are just turning soft. Different halves take different times to do this, anywhere between 5 and 10 minutes, so don't walk away and leave them – watch them carefully, and scoop them out individually and put them in a bowl when they are done.

When the apricot halves are all done, take out the vanilla bean, scrape out the seeds and put them back in the syrup.

Reduce the syrup by about half, then leave it to cool.

Pour the syrup over the apricots and add the blueberries, if you wish, at this point.

You can chill the compôte, but I love it warm, served with almond biscuits.

RHUBARB AND ORANGE

I was never very fond of rhubarb until Matthew, a fellow chef, suggested I bake it gently in the oven with orange zest and sugar, covered with foil. The rhubarb keeps its shape beautifully and the flavour of the orange complements it perfectly.

Serves 3–4
5 sticks (stems) rhubarb, trimmed and cut into 7 cm (3 inch) pieces
grated zest of 1 orange
about 150 g (¾ cup) caster (superfine) sugar
Crème Anglaise, to serve (see below)

Preheat the oven to 180°C/350°F/Gas Mark 4.

Place the rhubarb in a baking dish and mix in the orange zest and sugar according to taste. You will need to add a fair amount of sugar as this will lift the flavour of the fruit and provide a little syrup.

Cover with foil and bake in the oven for about 15 minutes. Check after 10 minutes as the cooking time depends on the quality of the rhubarb – it could be about 25 minutes. As soon as a knife slips easily into the fruit it is ready.

Chill.

This is lovely served with Crème Anglaise.

Variation
As we change our menu daily, depending on what is available and good, we sometimes add blueberries, strawberries or other types of fruit.

CRÈME ANGLAISE

Serves 4
250 ml (1 cup) single (light) cream
½ vanilla bean, halved lengthways to scatter the seeds
4 egg yolks
50 g (¼ cup) caster (superfine) sugar

Put the cream and vanilla bean in a saucepan and bring gently to the boil, then immediately remove from the heat.

In a bowl, beat the egg yolks with the sugar.

Tip some of the warm cream into the bowl to warm the eggs.

Pour the mixture back into the cream in the saucepan and stir gently with a wooden spoon over a very low heat until the cream coats the back of the spoon. This will take 2–5 minutes, depending on how hot the cream was to start with.

Strain into a jug and chill.

RHUBARB AND ORANGE, WITH ADDED BERRIES

POACHED PEACHES AND RED FRUITS

I really like a mixture of cooked and raw fruits, and the choices are great. The combination of apricots and blueberries in the **C**ompôte of Apricots and Vanilla (see page 42) is a favourite. For this recipe, try to get white peaches with very red skins.

Serves 4–6
200 g (1 cup) **caster** (superfine) **sugar**
juice of 2 lemons
6 red-skinned white peaches, halved and stoned
2 handfuls raspberries or blackberries

Put the sugar in a saucepan with **500 ml** (2 cups) water and bring to the boil over a gentle heat, stirring constantly until the sugar dissolves.

Add the lemon juice.

Add the peaches and poach gently until they are just soft–this could take about 10 minutes. The skins will turn the syrup beautifully pink, but they might slip off. If they do, just take them out.

When the peaches are done, remove any remaining skins, if you prefer.

Put the peaches in a bowl and, when the compôte is cool, add the raspberries or blackberries.

Serve at room temperature.

Variation
In winter, we poach pears instead of peaches, choosing varieties which keep their shape well, such as the **C**onference pear. **W**e sometimes serve these with a piece of shortbread on the side. The pears need to be poached for a little longer, about 15–20 minutes.

FRUIT TABOULÉ

This salad of grain and fruits is great for breakfast instead of muesli, and equally good as a dessert. You can use any fruits, fresh or dried. I have chosen ones that remind me of the areas where taboulé (or tabbouleh) is traditionally eaten, such as **N**orth Africa and the Middle East.

Serves 6
200 g (1 cup) **caster** (superfine) **sugar**
500 g (1 pound 2 ounces) **medium bulgar wheat**
200 ml (scant 1 cup) **apple or orange juice**
1 handful dates, stoned and chopped
2 apples, unpeeled and chopped
2 pears, peeled and chopped
1 large handful stewed apricots or figs
pinch of ground cinnamon
1 handful chopped fresh mint (optional)
sugar, honey or lemon juice, to taste

Put the sugar in a saucepan with **500 ml** (2 cups) water and bring to the boil over a gentle heat, stirring constantly until the sugar dissolves.

Set aside until the syrup is warm rather than hot.

Put the bulgar wheat in a bowl with the apple or orange juice and the warm syrup and leave to stand for about 2 hours, until all the moisture is absorbed and the bulgar wheat has softened.

Drain off any excess liquid.

Add the dates, apples, pears, apricots or figs, cinnamon, and the mint if you wish.

Mix well and add sugar, honey or lemon juice to taste.

Serve at room temperature.

Variation
You can use couscous instead of bulgar wheat if you prefer. Both are good.

POACHED PEARS, IDEAL FOR A FRUIT SALAD IN WINTER

At Rose Bakery our classic freshly squeezed juice is our Sunrise Juice, which is simply a mixture of pink grapefruit and oranges (blood oranges when in season) – combined, their colour reminds us of the sunrise... We also have on the menu a smoothie, to which we do not add crushed ice as they usually do in restaurants. So it is pure fruit and yogurt (or a non-dairy alternative). Of course, you are welcome to add the ice if you prefer its texture.

CLASSIC BANANA SMOOTHIE

Serves 1
1 banana
1 teaspoon honey
2 tablespoons apple juice
125 ml (½ cup) cup natural (plain) yogurt
  or soya (soy) milk

Put all the ingredients in a food processor and liquidize until smooth and frothy.

Serve immediately.

Variations
* Add a handful of strawberries in season.
* Replace the apple juice with lime juice, the honey with 1 tablespoon sugar and add a handful of desiccated (dried) or grated fresh coconut (grated fresh is better!).
* Replace the banana with soft chunks of mango and add a dash of lime juice to the apple juice.
* Use any poached fruit and some of its liquid, especially apricots, instead of the banana and you won't need the apple juice.
* A popular and different kind of smoothie is made with rice milk instead of yogurt. You then add a few chopped dates, a handful of oats and almonds, and a banana. And so on. If you wish.

LIME, GRAPEFRUIT AND GINGER JUICE

Serves 2
3 tablespoons caster (superfine) sugar, plus
  extra to taste
2 tablespoons grated fresh ginger
juice of 2 limes
juice of 2 grapefruit

Put the sugar in a small saucepan with 250 ml (1 cup) water and the ginger and simmer for about 5 minutes.

Take off the heat and allow to infuse and cool.

Strain into a jug and stir in the lime and grapefruit juices.

The juice should be sweet enough, but add extra sugar if you wish.

TOMATO, CELERY AND SPRING ONION (SCALLION) JUICE

Serves 2
4 ripe tomatoes, chopped
1 stick celery, chopped
2 spring onions (scallions), chopped
1 tablespoon concentrated tomato purée (paste)
1 teaspoon red or white wine vinegar
salt and pepper

Put all the ingredients in a food processor with 125 ml (½ cup) water and liquidize.

Taste and add more salt and pepper if needed.

Strain into two glasses.

CLASSIC BANANA SMOOTHIE

CEREALS

Our brunch menu includes two kinds of granola and a raw muesli. We also sell a lot of traditional porridge (using imported English organic oats). When we explain how simple it is to make porridge our customers can't believe it, so I have included the recipe here.

GRANOLA

We make two granolas, one that is sugar-free, sweetened with apple juice, and another made with honey and sugar. It is important to turn the granola frequently while it is baking, and watch it carefully as it can easily burn.
We often let it dry out overnight as the oven cools. This produces a crisper and dryer cereal. Do adjust the temperatures given in the recipe to your oven. The cereal must cook evenly and well enough for there to be no wet bits.

1. SUGAR-FREE GRANOLA

Serves 6
300 g (4 cups) **rolled oats**
100 g (1 cup) **whole almonds**
120 g (¾ cup) **sunflower seeds**
120 g (1 cup) **pumpkin seeds**
40 g (¼ cup) **sesame seeds**
1 tablespoon wheatgerm
125 ml (½ cup) **apple juice**
4 tablespoons sunflower oil
dried or fresh fruits, such as blueberries,
   strawberries or sultanas
natural (plain) **yogurt, to serve**

Preheat the oven to 160°C/325°F/Gas Mark 3.

Mix all the ingredients together in a bowl, then spread out evenly on a baking tray.

Bake, turning often, for between 45 minutes and 1 hour.

Remove from the oven and leave until cool.

Add the dried or fresh fruits and serve with yogurt.

2. HONEY GRANOLA

Serves 6
400 g (5⅓ cups) **rolled oats**
125 g (1¼ cups) **whole almonds**
100 g (⅔ cup) **sunflower seeds**
100 g (¾ cup) **pumpkin seeds**
50 g (⅓ cup) **sesame seeds**
1 tablespoon wheatgerm
125 ml (½ cup) **sunflower oil**
250 ml (1 cup) **honey**
50 g (¼ cup) **brown sugar**
a few drops of vanilla extract
pinch of ground cinnamon
½ teaspoon salt
1 handful dried fruit, such as sultanas
   (golden raisins) **or dates**
milk or soya (soy) **milk, to serve**

Preheat the oven to 160°C/325°F/Gas Mark 3.

In a bowl, mix together the oats, almonds, seeds and wheatgerm.

Put the sunflower oil, honey, sugar, vanilla, cinnamon and salt in a saucepan with **125 ml** (½ cup) **water.**

Bring just to the boil, stirring constantly, then pour over the dry ingredients in the bowl and mix well.

If the mixture is too wet add more oats – there should be no excess liquid at the bottom of the pan, and the mixture should be sticky.

Spread out evenly on a baking tray and bake slowly for about 1 hour.

Reduce the temperature to 140°C/275°F/Gas Mark 1 and continue baking until the granola is golden – about 1 hour.

Switch off the oven and leave to dry out for a further hour – or even overnight.

When all is cool and ready to eat, add the dried fruit, and serve with milk or soya milk.

HONEY GRANOLA

RAW MUESLI

We keep this healthy and nourishing dish simple, as it has always been, resisting the temptation to add different fruits. It is just so good as it is, all through the year.

Serves 4
150 g (2 cups) **rolled oats, soaked in** 250 ml (1 cup) **water or apple juice for about 1 hour, or even overnight**
125 ml (½ cup) **natural** (plain) **yogurt**
1 **apple, peeled or unpeeled, grated, plus extra to serve (optional)**
2 **heaped tablespoons chopped almonds**
1 **tablespoon wheatgerm**
1 **tablespoon honey, plus extra to serve (optional)**
pinch of ground cinnamon (optional)
1 **small handful sultanas** (golden raisins)

Mix all the ingredients together, then serve as we do – topped with extra grated apple and a little more honey if desired.

Wonderful. I can't think of a nicer way to start the day!

TRADITIONAL PORRIDGE

At Rose Bakery our staff love eating this with maple syrup and sliced bananas. It's a great, energizing start to a cold winter's day.

Serves 2
75 g (1 cup) **rolled oats**
pinch of salt

To serve
milk or cream, warmed
honey or brown sugar

Put the oats in a small saucepan with 500 ml (2 cups) **water** and slowly bring to the boil, stirring all the time.

Turn the heat down immediately, then add the salt – a vital ingredient!

Continue to stir well until the mixture thickens and becomes creamy. This will take anywhere between 5 and 15 minutes.

When you are satisfied that the texture is perfect, pour the porridge into a bowl and serve with warm milk or cream, and honey or brown sugar.

NOA, ONE OF OUR REGULARS

EGGS

The amount of eggs and bacon we sell at weekends is amazing, far beyond our expectations. Then again, our imported English bacon must seem very different from the kind that is available in Paris. There is nothing like eggs, tomatoes, mushrooms and good-quality crispy bacon at any time of the day, and I understand why people enjoy them. I have not included a recipe for bacon and eggs as everyone knows how they like theirs cooked and can easily achieve it!

PERFECT SCRAMBLED EGGS

I feel a bit silly giving a recipe for scrambled eggs, as they really are so simple and basic and everyone cooks them in a different way. However, if you want them creamy but well cooked – as I like them – here is how we do them.

Serves 1
3 eggs, organic if possible
1 tablespoon double (heavy) cream
salt and ground black pepper
knob (pat) of unsalted butter
1 or 2 slices of smoked salmon, to serve

In a bowl, beat the eggs with the cream and a pinch each of salt and pepper.

Melt the butter in a non-stick saucepan over a low heat.

When the butter has just melted, add the eggs, and keep stirring until they are not runny any more, and are completely cooked but with a very creamy texture.

Place the eggs and salmon on a plate and serve immediately as the eggs will continue cooking.

Variations
Serve the eggs with:
* Chopped chives and parsley
* Cooked chorizo on the side
* Bread croûtons
* Slow-roasted tomatoes. Roast at 180°C/350°F/Gas Mark 4 for about 45 minutes, depending on the water content of the tomatoes
* Simply on buttered toast, the English way

FRESH EGGS FOR BREAKFAST

PANCAKES

Pancakes are on the brunch menu every weekend, whether served with bacon and maple syrup or fruit. I have included just some of the ones we do, as the possibilities are endless, and so too are the fruit toppings. Like bacon and eggs, pancakes are so popular I know I will be making many people happy by giving these recipes. The important thing to remember when making pancakes is never to overmix the batter. Once the wet is added to the dry, you must turn the batter over with a large spoon no more than eight times!

CLASSIC PANCAKES

At Rose Bakery we often serve these pancakes with sliced bananas, or we sprinkle blueberries over the pancakes in the pan just before we turn them over.

Serves 4–6
2 eggs
220 ml (scant 1 cup) **milk**
5 tablespoons unsalted butter, melted,
    plus a little for cooking
190 g (scant 1¼ cups) **plain** (all-purpose) **flour**
½ teaspoon salt
1 tablespoon caster (superfine) sugar
4 teaspoons baking powder
maple syrup and your choice of fruit, to serve

In a bowl, beat the eggs with the milk and melted butter. Put aside.

In another bowl, sift together the flour with the salt, sugar and baking powder.

Pour the egg mixture into the flour and stir very lightly until the wet and dry ingredients are just combined.

Rub a small frying pan with a little butter, heat the pan to hot and pour in 3–4 tablespoons of batter.

Tilt the pan so that the batter covers the base evenly and turn the heat down to medium.

Cook until a few bubbles come to the surface and then turn the pancake over.

Cook for about another minute.

Continue making pancakes until all the batter is used up, adding more butter as necessary.

Serve immediately, as pancakes are best eaten hot, with maple syrup and fruit.

RICOTTA PANCAKES

When we have too much fresh ricotta cheese from Italy we make these wonderful pancakes, and serve them with honey, maple syrup or fresh red-fruit compôtes.

Serves 8
200 g (scant 1 cup) **ricotta cheese**
190 ml (¾ cup) **milk**
4 eggs, separated
150 g (1 cup) **plain** (all-purpose) **flour**
1 teaspoon baking powder
½ teaspoon salt
a little unsalted butter, for cooking
your choice of sweet sauce and fruit, to serve

In a bowl, beat the ricotta with the milk and egg yolks until smooth.

In another bowl, sift together the flour and the baking powder and salt.

Add the ricotta mixture to the flour and stir very lightly.

Beat the egg whites until they are stiff and carefully fold them into the batter.

Melt a piece of the butter in a small frying pan, pour in 3–4 tablespoons of batter and tilt the pan so that the batter covers the base evenly.

Cook over a low to medium heat until the pancake is lightly golden underneath.

Turn over and cook for about another minute until the pancake is cooked through.

Continue making pancakes until all the batter is used up, adding more butter as necessary.

Serve hot with a sweet sauce and fruit.

CLASSIC PANCAKES

GLUTEN-FREE BUCKWHEAT PANCAKES

Every so often we are asked to do gluten-free pancakes, so we have come up with these buckwheat ones. Buckwheat is not related to the wheat family, and is in fact a wild herb that originated in Russia and central Asia. It is extremely hardy and can grow anywhere, and has therefore been grown organically for a long time, making it a naturally healthy food. If it is used on its own, however, it can make the pancakes quite heavy, so we mix it with other gluten-free flours.

Serves 4–6
4 eggs, separated
400 ml (1¾ cups) **milk**
100 ml (scant ½ cup) **natural** (plain) **yogurt**
150 g (1 cup) **buckwheat flour**
70 g (½ cup) **rice flour**
2 tablespoons cornmeal
1 teaspoon baking powder
pinch of salt
a little unsalted butter, for cooking
2 tablespoons caster (superfine) sugar
your choice of sweet sauce and fruit, to serve

In a bowl, beat the egg yolks, milk and yogurt until smooth.

In another bowl, sift together the buckwheat and rice flours and the cornmeal, baking powder, sugar and salt.

Add the milk mixture to the flours and stir very lightly.

Beat the egg whites until they are stiff and carefully fold them into the batter.

Melt a piece of the butter in a small frying pan, pour in 3–4 tablespoons of batter and tilt the pan so that the batter covers the base evenly.

Cook over a low to medium heat until the pancake is lightly golden underneath.

Turn over and cook for about another minute until the pancake is cooked through.

Continue making pancakes until all the batter is used up, adding more butter as necessary.

Serve hot with a sweet sauce and fruit.

VEGAN PANCAKES

This is our recipe for dairy-free pancakes.

Serves 4–6
5 tablespoons sunflower oil, plus extra
  for cooking
250 ml (1 cup) **soya** (soy) **milk or water**
150 g (1 cup) **plain** (all-purpose) **flour**
40 g (¼ cup) **wholemeal** (wholewheat) **flour**
1 tablespoon caster (superfine) sugar
3 teaspoons baking powder
pinch of salt
your choice of sweet sauce and fruit, to serve

In a bowl, mix the oil and soya milk.

In another bowl, sift together the plain and wholemeal flours and the baking powder, sugar and salt.

Add the milk mixture to the flours and stir very lightly.

Melt a little oil in a small frying pan, pour in 3–4 tablespoons of batter and tilt the pan so that the batter covers the base evenly.

Cook over a low to medium heat until the pancake is lightly golden underneath.

Turn over and cook for about another minute until the pancake is cooked through.

Continue making pancakes until all the batter is used up, adding more oil as necessary.

Serve hot with a sweet sauce and fruit.

MAKING PANCAKE BATTER

SCONES

It was a wonderful surprise to discover how much the French love scones. We sell far more of them in Paris than we ever did in London. One of our regular customers has said that her child will only eat our scones, nothing else! My scones are a little bit «unsconelike» in appearance as I have changed the traditional recipes into something lighter – like rock cakes but softer. This may make the shapes a little wilder, but texture won the battle over tradition!

PLAIN SCONES

Makes 12–15 scones
500 g (3⅓ cups) **plain** (all-purpose) **flour, plus extra for dusting**
1 handful wheatgerm or wholemeal (wholewheat) **flour or cornmeal (optional)**
2 very heaped tablespoons baking powder
2 heaped tablespoons caster (superfine) **sugar**
1 teaspoon salt
110 g (scant ½ cup) **unsalted butter, cut into pieces, plus extra for greasing**
about 300 ml (1¼ cups) **whole, semi-skimmed or soya** (soy) **milk**
1 egg, beaten
butter and jam, to serve

Preheat the oven to 200°C/400°F/Gas Mark 6 and grease a baking tray with butter, or use baking parchment.

Sift the plain flour into a bowl and add the wheatgerm or wholemeal flour or cornmeal, if using.

Mix in the baking powder, sugar and salt, then add the butter and rub in with your fingers until the mixture resembles fresh breadcrumbs.

Make a well in the middle, pour in exactly 300 ml (1¼ cups) **milk and use a fork to work it into the dry ingredients.**

Finish by hand but without overworking the mixture – just lightly bring everything together to form a softish but firm dough.

If it is too dry add a little more milk, and if it is too wet add some more flour. It must not be sticky at all.

On a lightly floured surface, pat or roll the dough into a solid shape about 3 cm (1¼ inches) **thick.**

Using a 5 cm (2 inch) **cutter, cut the dough into rounds and place them on the greased baking tray so that they almost touch.**

Glaze the tops with the beaten egg, and bake for 15–20 minutes until lightly golden.

The scones will stick together, so take them gently apart when they have cooled a little.

Serve warm with butter and jam.

MAKING SCONES

SULTANA (GOLDEN RAISIN) SCONES

Makes 12–15 scones
500 g (3⅓ cups) **plain** (all-purpose) **flour, plus extra for dusting**
1 handful wheatgerm or wholemeal (wholewheat) **flour or cornmeal (optional)**
2 very heaped tablespoons baking powder
2 heaped tablespoons caster (superfine) **sugar**
1 teaspoon salt
110 g (scant ½ cup) **unsalted butter, cut into pieces, plus extra for greasing**
160 g (1 cup) **sultanas** (golden raisins), **soaked in orange juice if you wish**
about 300 ml (1¼ cups) **whole, semi-skimmed or soya** (soy) **milk**
1 egg, beaten
butter and jam, to serve

Preheat the oven to 200°C/400°F/Gas Mark 6 and grease a baking tray with butter.

Sift the plain flour into a bowl and add the wheatgerm or wholemeal flour or cornmeal, if using.

Mix in the baking powder, sugar and salt, then add the butter and rub in with your fingers until the mixture resembles fresh breadcrumbs.

Add the sultanas and mix well.

Make a well in the middle, pour in exactly 300 ml (1¼ cups) milk and use a fork to work it into the dry ingredients. Finish by hand but without overworking the mixture – just lightly bring everything together to form a softish but firm dough. If it is too dry add a little more milk, and if it is too wet add some more flour. It must not be sticky at all.

On a lightly floured surface, pat or roll the dough into a solid shape about 3 cm (1¼ inches) thick.

Using a 5 cm (2 inch) cutter, cut the dough into rounds and place them on the greased baking tray so that they almost touch.

Glaze the tops with the beaten egg, and bake for 15–20 minutes until lightly golden.

The scones will stick together, so take them gently apart when they have cooled a little.

Serve warm with butter and jam.

BLUEBERRY SCONES

These are really popular at Rose Bakery. I've tried other berries but they all turn the scone dough into a sticky mess. Blueberries, on the other hand, don't crush as much and keep their shape, but it is important to handle the dough extra carefully.

Makes 12–15 scones
500 g (3⅓ cups) **plain** (all-purpose) **flour, plus extra for dusting**
1 handful wheatgerm or wholemeal (wholewheat) **flour or cornmeal (optional)**
2 very heaped tablespoons baking powder
2 heaped tablespoons caster (superfine) **sugar**
1 teaspoon salt
grated zest of 1 lemon or 1 orange
110 g (scant ½ cup) **unsalted butter, cut into pieces, plus extra for greasing**
2 handfuls blueberries
2 eggs
about 300 ml (1¼ cups) **whole, semi-skimmed or soya** (soy) **milk**
1 tablespoon demerara (light brown) **sugar**
crème fraîche (sour cream), **to serve**

Preheat the oven to 200°C/400°F/Gas Mark 6 and grease a baking tray with butter.

Sift the plain flour into a bowl and add the wheatgerm or wholemeal flour or cornmeal, if using.

Mix in the baking powder, caster sugar and salt, then add the butter and rub in with your fingers until the mixture resembles fresh breadcrumbs.

Mix in the lemon or orange zest.

Add the blueberries and mix well.

Beat one of the eggs in a measuring jug, then add enough milk to reach the 300 ml (1¼ cup) level.

Make a well in the middle, pour in the liquid and use a fork to work it into the dry ingredients. Finish by hand but without overworking the mixture – just lightly bring everything together to form a softish but firm dough. If it is too dry add a little more milk, and if it is too wet add some more flour. It must not be sticky at all.

On a lightly floured surface, pat or roll the dough into a solid shape about 3 cm (1¼ inches) thick.

Using a 5 cm (2 inch) cutter, cut the dough into rounds and place them on the greased baking tray so that they almost touch.

Beat the remaining egg and use to glaze the tops of the scones.

Sprinkle with the demerara sugar and bake for 15–20 minutes until lightly golden.

The scones will stick together, so take them gently apart when they have cooled a little.

Serve warm with crème fraîche.

BLUEBERRY SCONES

MAPLE SYRUP SCONES

The smell of these when they are just out of the oven is heaven, and this has to be my favourite scone recipe. As they are already quite rich in butter I eat them with just a little jam, but Jean-Charles still melts large dollops of butter on them. My daughter, Marissa, loves hers with Marmite!

Makes 10–12 scones
260 g (1¾ cups) **plain** (all-purpose) **flour, plus** extra for dusting
80 g (½ cup) **wholemeal** (wholewheat) **flour**
35 g (½ cup) **rolled oats**
1 very heaped tablespoon baking powder
1 very heaped tablespoon caster (superfine) **sugar**
½ teaspoon salt
160 g (scant ¾ cup) **unsalted butter, cut into** pieces, plus extra for greasing
4 tablespoons maple syrup
about 4 tablespoons milk (or buttermilk)
1 egg, beaten

Preheat the oven to 200°C/400°F/Gas Mark 6 and grease a baking tray with butter.

Sift the plain and wholemeal flours into a bowl and mix in the oats, baking powder, sugar and salt.

Add the butter and rub in with your fingers until the mixture resembles fresh breadcrumbs.

In another bowl, mix together the syrup and 4 tablespoons milk or buttermilk.

Make a well in the middle of the flours and oats and pour in the syrup and milk mixture. Use a fork to work it into the dry ingredients. Finish by hand but without overworking the mixture – just lightly bring everything together to form a softish but firm dough. If it is too dry add a little more milk, and if it is too wet add some more flour. It must not be sticky at all.

On a lightly floured surface, pat or roll the dough into a solid shape about 3 cm (1¼ inches) thick.

Using a 5 cm (2 inch) cutter, cut the dough into rounds and place them on the greased baking tray so that they almost touch.

Glaze the tops with the beaten egg, and bake for 20–25 minutes until lightly golden.

The scones will stick together, so take them gently apart when they have cooled a little.

Serve warm. Enjoy and breathe in deeply!

DATE SCONES

These scones need to be served warm, just with lots of butter, and eaten slowly – if that's possible!

Makes 10 scones
250 g (1⅔ cups) **self-raising** (self-rising) **flour,** half white and half wholemeal (wholewheat), plus extra for dusting
¼ teaspoon ground nutmeg or mixed spice
pinch of salt
1 teaspoon baking powder
60 g (5 tablespoons) **unsalted butter, plus extra** for greasing
2 heaped tablespoons light brown sugar
250 g (scant ½ cup) **stoned, chopped dates**
150 ml (⅔ cup) **milk**
1 egg, beaten

Preheat the oven to 200°C/400°F/Gas Mark 6 and grease a baking tray with butter.

Sift the flours into a bowl with the nutmeg or mixed spice, salt and baking powder.

Add the butter and sugar and rub in with your fingers until the mixture resembles fresh breadcrumbs, then fold in the dates.

Make a well in the middle of the mixture and pour in the milk. Use a fork to work it into the dry ingredients. Finish by hand but without overworking the mixture – just lightly bring everything together to form a softish but firm dough. It must not be sticky, so start by adding three-quarters of the milk and see how that works. Add more only if you need it.

On a lightly floured surface, pat or roll the dough into a solid shape about 3 cm (1¼ inches) thick.

Cut the dough into rounds or squares and place them on the greased baking tray so that they almost touch.

Glaze the tops with the egg and bake for about 15 minutes until lightly golden.

The scones will stick together, so take them gently apart when they have cooled a little.

Serve warm.

BAKED SCONES ON THE COUNTER

CHEDDAR CORNMEAL SCONES

These golden yellow scones are great for people who prefer an unsweetened scone experience, or for serving with soup. We use a slightly bigger cutter for these scones, and also roll the dough a little thinner than for the other versions.

Makes 8–10 scones
200 g (1⅓ cups) **plain** (all-purpose) **flour**
130 g (1 cup) **cornmeal**
1 tablespoon polenta
1 very heaped tablespoon baking powder
1 heaped tablespoon caster (superfine) **sugar**
½ teaspoon salt
pinch of cayenne pepper
120 g (½ cup) **unsalted butter, cut into pieces, plus extra for greasing**
130 g (1⅓ cups) **grated Cheddar cheese**
3 small eggs
100 ml (scant ½ cup) **milk**

Preheat the oven to 200°C/400°F/Gas Mark 6 and grease a baking tray with butter.

Sift the plain flour into a bowl and mix with the cornmeal, polenta, baking powder, sugar, salt and cayenne.

Add the butter and rub in with your fingers until the mixture resembles fresh breadcrumbs, then mix in the Cheddar cheese.

In another bowl, beat two of the eggs and mix together with the milk.

Make a well in the middle of the flour and pour in the egg-and-milk mixture. Use a fork to work it into the dry ingredients. Finish by hand but without overworking the mixture – just lightly bring everything together to form a softish but firm dough. If it is too dry add a little more milk, and if it is too wet add some more flour. It must not be sticky at all.

On a lightly floured surface, pat or roll the dough into a solid shape about 2 cm (1 inch) **thick.**

Using a 6 cm (2¼ inch) **cutter, cut the dough into rounds and place them on the greased baking tray so that they almost touch.**

Glaze the tops with the third beaten egg, and bake for 20–25 minutes until lightly golden.

The scones will stick together, so take them gently apart when they have cooled a little.

Serve warm.

BEATEN EGG FOR GLAZING SCONES

LUNCH

THE COUNTER AT MIDDAY

SOUPS

GREEN BEAN AND ALMOND SOUP
SPICED CHICKPEA AND LEMON SOUP
CELERIAC AND PORCINI SOUP
COLD BEETROOT SOUP WITH A HOT POTATO
CRUSHED POTATO, CELERY AND HERB SOUP

SALADS

CARROT AND SEED SALAD
KOHLRABI, CUCUMBER AND MUSTARD CRESS SALAD
MUSHROOM, CELERY AND SPRING ONION SALAD
QUINOA AND PEPPER SALAD
POTATO GRIBICHE

PASTRY

SHORTCRUST PASTRY
VEGETABLE TARTS
MUSHROOM AND CHIVE TART
ARTICHOKE AND PEA TART
RICOTTA, TOMATO AND THYME TART
ONION PISSALADIÈRE
PIZZETTE

RISOTTOS

TOMATO, AUBERGINE AND MINT RISOTTO
COURGETTE AND MILLET RISOTTO
MUSHROOM AND PORCINI RISOTTO

MAIN COURSES

COD IN TOMATO WATER
BRAISED ARTICHOKE, LEMON AND LAMB CHOPS
ASPARAGUS AND ALMOND SALAD WITH CHICKEN
FISH BALLS IN BROTH
SALMON FILLETS AND BROCCOLI
BRAISED LAMB SHANKS WITH CUMIN, AUBERGINE AND CHICKPEAS

ROSE BAKERY
SATURDAY BRUNCH

25 Mars 2006

sunrise orange/pamplemouse, frais presse	4.00
compote fruits saison	6.00
banana smoothie (soya ou yaourt)	6.00
raw muesli (avec pommes, amandes, yaourt et miel)	7.50
traditional porridge with honey or brown sugar	6.50
oeufs a la coque avec 'toast marmite'	5.50
pancakes au banane, syrop d'erable	8.50
fried ricotta et salade mixte	10.00
eggs bacon tomato and mushroom	12.50
saumon fume Bio d'Irlande, oeufs brouilles	14.50
soupe lentilles rouges au curry	6.00
tarte chaude/ pizzette, salade verte	9.00
tarte chaude/ pizzette, une salade du comptoir	11.50
crudites-legumes du comptoir (small 9.00)	13.00
poulet braise au tomate et cepes, avec polenta	14.00
salade verte Bio	4.00
fromage anglais (de Neals yard) et chutney RB	9.50
crumble aux pommes et rhubarbe	6.00
scones ou toast avec confiture et beurre	3.50
yaourt et miel	4.00
patisseries du comptoir au choix	4.00-7.00

pain jeanluc poilaran

As our products are bought from 'biologique' sources where possible, or from small traditional producers.

Il est recommande de ne pas fumer, vous mangez dans un etablissement de production de patisserie. Merci.

[...] produits du comptoir consommes sur glace seront majores de 50%

OUR BRUNCH MENU

LIGHT LUNCHES

By midday our counter is full of salads, quiches, pizzette, cakes and pastries. The display is different every day, and is mouthwatering and delightful. The menu for eat-in food is kept very simple as most customers choose from the counter, and that is how it is supposed to be. We succumbed to the pressure of adding a «formule» to our menu. It is not something I have ever done before, as I feel there is enough choice, at good prices, on the menu and at the counter. But somehow it has become the way to eat lunch for many people in France and who am I to try to change that!

During the week, there are queues from midday until 3pm for the counter food as well as the restaurant, but we often find ourselves having to turn people away as there simply isn't enough space to seat them all. However, weekdays are still very different from the mayhem of weekends, a little more civilized and quieter. The place is usually completely crazy at the weekends, with a huge number of babies and small children, and the noise of families getting together for Sunday brunch or lunch. I think one of the reasons we have so many families coming to Rose Bakery is our non-smoking policy, but our area in the 9th arrondissement is also becoming increasingly popular with young families, and that is wonderful. We also have many regular customers who come practically every day. As soon as they walk in the door, we know what they will have and how they will want it – no starch; only the vegetables; no chickpeas, please; just a salad on the side; soup but no green bits on top...

There is always a soup on the menu, through winter and summer. And even on the hottest of days, when the last thing on your mind is soup, and you've climbed the steep rue des Martyrs to where we are, it still sells. Our list of soups is endless, but here are the favourites.

GREEN BEAN AND ALMOND SOUP

We sometimes make the stock for this (and our other soups) with Marigold bouillon powder, found in good wholefood stores and some supermarkets. Use about 1 teaspoon to 1 litre (4 cups) **water.**

Serves 6
4 tablespoons extra virgin olive oil
2 onions, diced
2 sticks celery, diced
2 carrots, diced
1 garlic clove, crushed
1 teaspoon salt
pinch of ground black pepper
1 teaspoon caster (superfine) **sugar (optional)**
500 g (1 pound 2 ounces) **green beans, trimmed (or 3 large handfuls)**
about 1 litre (4 cups) **vegetable stock (see above) or water, i.e. enough stock or water to cover the vegetables by 3 cm** (1¼ inches)
100 g (1 cup) **ground almonds**

Heat the oil in a saucepan, and cook the onions, celery, carrots and garlic over a low heat, stirring occasionally, until the vegetables soften and are beginning to turn golden.

Add the salt and pepper. Getting the vegetables this good and flavourful at the start is the secret of the best soups. I sometimes add some sugar at this stage.

Add the beans and stir well for about 5 minutes.

Pour in the stock or water – the liquid should cover the vegetables by about 3 cm (1¼ inches).

Simmer for about 30 minutes till all the vegetables are soft.

Add the almonds. Stir well, take off the heat and leave to cool slightly.

Transfer to a food processor and liquidize until smooth. If the soup is too thick add a little more stock or water.

Taste and season if necessary.

SPICED CHICKPEA (GARBANZO BEAN) AND LEMON SOUP

I love chickpeas (garbanzo beans) in all their forms, and this soup is one of my favourites. It is a soup for winter and summer.

Serves 6
370 g (2 cups) chickpeas (garbanzo beans), soaked overnight in 1 litre (4 cups) water to which a pinch of bicarbonate of soda (baking soda) has been added
4 tablespoons extra virgin olive oil
2 onions, diced
2 sticks celery, diced
1 carrot, diced
2 garlic cloves, crushed
1 teaspoon salt
pinch of ground black pepper
1 tablespoon ground cumin
1 dried red chilli (chile), crushed
about 1½ litres (6 cups) vegetable stock (made with 1 teaspoon Marigold bouillon powder to 1 litre (4 cups) water, if you wish) or water
pinch of Marigold bouillon powder (optional)
2 tablespoons lemon juice
pinch of sugar

To garnish
6 lemon wedges and chopped fresh coriander (cilantro) leaves; or a sprinkling of freshly roasted cumin seeds and sesame seeds, ground or whole

Drain the chickpeas and put them in a saucepan with enough cold water to cover.

Bring to the boil, then simmer till soft – anywhere between 1 and 2 hours – skimming the surface as necessary.

Towards the end of the cooking time, heat the oil in another saucepan and cook the onions, celery and carrot over a low heat, stirring occasionally, till the vegetables soften and are just beginning to turn golden.

Add the garlic, salt, pepper, ground cumin and chilli. Stir for a few minutes, then add the chickpeas and enough chickpea liquid and stock or water to cover the vegetables by about 3 cm (1¼ inches).

Simmer for about 30 minutes, then transfer to a food processor and liquidize to a smooth light purée. Add more stock or water if the soup is too thick.

Taste and season if necessary. I sometimes add a little Marigold bouillon powder if it is too bland. I also add lemon juice and a pinch of sugar.

Garnish with lemon wedges and coriander leaves, or a sprinkling of cumin seeds and sesame seeds.

CELERIAC AND PORCINI SOUP

The combination of celeriac and porcini mushrooms, also known as ceps, is so good. We don't put cream in our soups but this one could take a little if you wish.

Serves 6
1 large handful dried porcini, soaked in 400 ml (1¾ cups) hot water for 30 minutes
4 tablespoons extra virgin olive oil
2 medium onions, diced
2 sticks celery, diced
1 carrot, diced
2 garlic cloves, crushed
1 teaspoon salt
pinch of ground black pepper
1 dried red chilli (chile), crushed
500 g (1 pound 2 ounces) celeriac (celery root), diced
about 1 litre (4 cups) vegetable stock (made with 1 teaspoon Marigold bouillon powder to 1 litre (4 cups) water, if you wish) or water

Strain the porcini and reserve the soaking liquid. Set both aside.

Heat the oil in a saucepan and cook the onions, celery, carrot, garlic, salt, pepper and chilli over a low heat, stirring occasionally, until the vegetables soften and are beginning to turn golden.

Add the celeriac and stir for a few minutes, then add the porcini, their strained soaking liquid and enough stock or water to come at least 3 cm (1¼ inches) above the vegetables. Simmer for about 40 minutes.

Transfer to a food processor and liquidize to a smooth light purée.

Taste and season if necessary.

COLD BEETROOT SOUP
WITH A HOT POTATO

COLD BEETROOT (BEET) SOUP WITH A HOT POTATO

This soup is based on the classic Lithuanian borscht, and our customers find the combination of hot and cold surprising but delicious. It needs to be chilled overnight, so remember to prepare the borscht the day before you plan to serve it.

Serves 6
2 onions, diced
2 sticks celery, diced
1 kg (2 pounds 2 ounces) raw beetroot (beet), peeled and diced
about 2 litres (8 cups) water
salt and ground black pepper
1 tablespoon red or white wine vinegar or lemon juice
2 tablespoons caster (superfine) sugar
6 medium potatoes, washed and not peeled
soured (sour) cream, to garnish

Put the onions, celery and beetroot in a large saucepan and cover well with about 2 litres (8 cups) water.

Season with salt and pepper.

Bring to the boil and simmer for about 2 hours till the beetroot is soft.

Transfer to a food processor and liquidize to make a very thin purée. If the soup is too thick add more water.

Chill overnight.

Next day add the vinegar or lemon juice, and sugar. Check for seasoning. The soup must have a slightly sweet / sour taste.

Boil the potatoes until soft, then halve them.

Pour the cold soup into bowls, put two hot potato halves in the middle of each bowl and add a good spoonful of soured cream to each serving.

CRUSHED POTATO, CELERY AND HERB SOUP

You will need floury (mealy) potatoes for this soup, as waxy new ones will not crush. The soup isn't liquidized, so make sure the onions and celery are finely diced.

Serves 6
4 tablespoons extra virgin olive oil
3 onions, finely diced
3 sticks celery, finely diced
1 teaspoon salt
pinch of ground black pepper
1 garlic clove, crushed
600 g (1 pound 3 ounces) potatoes, peeled and diced
1½ litres (6 cups) vegetable stock (made with 1 teaspoon Marigold bouillon powder to 1 litre (4 cups) water, if you wish) or water
2 handfuls chopped fresh parsley
2 handfuls chopped fresh chives
pinch of fresh thyme

To garnish
extra virgin olive oil
a sprinkling of chopped fresh parsley and chives (optional)

Heat the oil in a saucepan and cook the onions, celery, salt, pepper and garlic over a low heat, stirring occasionally, till the vegetables are soft but not coloured.

Add the potatoes, cover well with stock or water and simmer for about 30 minutes.

When the potatoes are soft take the saucepan off the heat and use a fork to crush them. Using a fork is crucial as we are not looking for a smooth soup – it must be textured.

Add the parsley, chives and thyme.

Heat for another 10 minutes to soften the herbs.

Taste and season if necessary.

Garnish with a swirl of oil and, if you wish, a sprinkling of chopped herbs.

THE LUNCHTIME RUSH

SALADS

For many people a salad, raw or cooked, is a daily essential. It can start a meal or may even be the whole meal, so important has it become. Every day at Rose Bakery, therefore, we produce six to eight salads that can either be eaten individually or composed as a plate of crudités. We approach each salad differently, deciding how to cook this vegetable or slice that one. The way a vegetable is cooked (roasted, grilled, blanched) varies from day to day, season to season. How it is sliced affects the taste, texture and balance of the dish. I prefer my carrots grated; my daughter cuts hers into small chunks – same salad, different taste and experience! These recipes are guidelines only – even as I write them, I am changing them…

We used to have white cardboard boxes for our take-out salads, as seen in the photograph on page 83, but we have recently started using amazing new containers that look like plastic but are actually made from maize – biodegradable and all. When we first introduced them, one of our customers was horrified, and couldn't believe we would use plastic. We told her about the material, and now she is trying it out on her compost heap. So far, so good. We are waiting for her report.

DRESSINGS

When making a dressing always add the oil at the end, after you have mixed the lemon juice or vinegars and seasonings. And taste for seasoning and balance before you add the oil. It is too late for any serious seasoning after it has been added.

THE SALAD COUNTER, INCLUDING
CARROT AND SEED SALAD

CARROT AND SEED SALAD

Any carrot salad has to be my favourite, but ever since the day when my assistant, Alice, suggested we use sunflower seeds as well as herbs, we have never looked back. I can't decide whether I prefer sunflower or pumpkin seeds, so the recipe gives both. Try either, and make up your own mind.

Serves 6
130 g (1 cup) **sunflower or pumpkin seeds**
1 tablespoon **sunflower or rapeseed** (canola) **oil (optional)**
pinch of salt
8 **medium carrots, grated**
1 **handful chopped chives**

For the dressing
125 ml (½ cup) **lemon juice**
1 **teaspoon salt**
½ **teaspoon ground black pepper**
1 **tablespoon caster** (superfine) **sugar**
about 3 tablespoons sunflower oil or olive oil

Preheat the oven to 180°C/350°F/Gas Mark 4 and, if you wish, mix the seeds with the oil.

Season the seeds with the salt, spread them evenly on a baking tray and bake for approximately 15 minutes till they are lightly roasted and crisp, turning frequently. Set aside to cool.

Place the carrots in a serving bowl.

To make the dressing, whisk together the lemon juice, salt, pepper and sugar in a bowl, then whisk in the oil. Check the seasoning – you may need more salt, sugar or lemon juice.

Pour the dressing over the carrots and mix well.

Sprinkle with the chives and the cooled seeds.

KOHLRABI, CUCUMBER AND MUSTARD CRESS SALAD

Serves 6
1 **cucumber**
6 **medium kohlrabis, cut into matchstick slices**
2–3 **punnets or about** 150 g (3 cups) **mustard and cress (or any other sprouted seed)**

For the dressing
50 ml (¼ cup) **white wine vinegar**
½ **teaspoon salt**
pinch of ground black pepper
pinch of cayenne pepper
pinch of sugar
1 **tablespoon Dijon mustard**
50 ml (¼ cup) **sunflower or rapeseed** (canola) **oil**
50 ml (¼ cup) **extra virgin olive oil**

Half-peel the cucumber, alternating stripes of peel and flesh, then halve it lengthways, take out the seeds and cut it into 5 mm (¼ inch) slices.

Place in a serving bowl and mix with the kohlrabis.

To make the dressing, whisk together the vinegar, salt, black pepper, cayenne, sugar and mustard in a bowl. Whisk in the oils and check the seasoning.

Pour the dressing over the cucumber and kohlrabi and mix well.

Finally, gently fold in the mustard and cress.

Serve immediately.

MUSHROOM, CELERY AND SPRING ONION
(SCALLION) **SALAD**

Serves 6
2 tablespoons extra virgin olive oil
500 g (7¼ cups) **mushrooms, sliced**
pinch each of salt and ground black pepper
1 garlic clove, crushed
1 celery heart (the inner yellow part),
  finely sliced
3 spring onions (scallions), **sliced at 45 degrees**
1 large handful fresh coriander (cilantro) **leaves,
  coarsely chopped, to garnish**

For the dressing
125 ml (½ cup) **lime juice**
1 Thai chilli (chile), **finely chopped**
½ teaspoon salt
pinch of ground black pepper
pinch of sugar
1 garlic clove, crushed
125 ml (½ cup) **sunflower or rapeseed**
  (canola) **oil**

Heat the oil in a frying pan and cook the
mushrooms over a high heat with the salt,
pepper and garlic until almost all the liquid
has gone. Set aside and leave to cool.

In a serving bowl, mix the celery and spring
onions with the cooled mushrooms.

To make the dressing, whisk together the
lime juice, chilli, salt, pepper, sugar and
garlic in a bowl. Whisk in the oil and check
the seasoning.

Pour the dressing over the salad, mix well
and sprinkle with coriander.

QUINOA AND PEPPER
(BELL PEPPER) **SALAD**

Serves 6
170 g (1 cup) quinoa
salt and ground black pepper
4 tablespoons extra virgin olive oil
1 red, 1 green and 1 yellow pepper (bell pepper),
  finely diced
2 medium onions, finely diced
1 courgette (zucchini), **finely diced**
2 garlic cloves, crushed
1 dried red pepper (bell pepper), **crushed**
pinch of ground cumin (optional)
dash of lemon juice (optional)
chopped fresh parsley or coriander (cilantro),
  to garnish

Put the quinoa in a saucepan with 500 ml (2 cups)
water and a pinch of salt.

Bring to the boil, then turn the heat down to a
simmer and cook for about 15 minutes, until the
quinoa is soft and the water has been absorbed.
Set aside.

To make the sauce, heat the oil in a saucepan
and cook the peppers, onions and courgette
over a medium heat with a pinch each of salt
and black pepper, and the garlic and dried
red pepper.

Keep stirring until the mixture just begins to
turn soft—the vegetables must not soften too
much—and the colours blend into the oil.

Check the seasoning (you can add a little
cumin or lemon juice if you wish).

Pour the sauce into the quinoa and mix well.

Garnish with parsley or coriander and serve
warm or allow to cool to room temperature.

POTATO GRIBICHE

The list of potato salads is endless, and we do several versions including a classic boiled potato and mixed herb salad. One of our most popular ones, this is great with cold meats or on its own.

Serves 6
1.5 kg (3 pounds 3 ounces) **new potatoes, half peeled, alternating stripes of peel and flesh**
olive oil, for drizzling
salt and ground black pepper
3 large handfuls coarsely chopped flat-leaf parsley

For the dressing
4 hard-boiled (hard-cooked) **eggs, chopped**
100 g (3 ounces) **gherkins** (dill pickles)**, finely chopped**
2 tablespoons capers, chopped
2–3 shallots, finely chopped
pinch each of salt and ground black pepper
2 tablespoons red wine vinegar
1 teaspoon Dijon mustard
125 ml (½ cup) **extra virgin olive oil**

Preheat the oven to 220°C/425°F/Gas Mark 7.

Put the potatoes in a saucepan with cold water to cover, bring them to the boil and then drain them immediately.

Place on a baking tray and, while still hot, drizzle with a little oil and sprinkle with salt and pepper.

Roast till golden, about 1½ hours, but check after 50 minutes.

To make the dressing, combine all the ingredients and mix well.

When the potatoes are ready, place them in a serving bowl whilst still warm (this allows them to absorb the flavours of the dressing), fold in the dressing and mix in the parsley.

Serve slightly warm or cold.

Variations
Add to the basic recipe:
* 400 g (14 ounces) **chorizo, chopped. Add to the potatoes for the last 5 minutes of roasting, then mix well so all the flavours combine**
* 4 red peppers (bell peppers)**, cut into large pieces and added to the potatoes on the baking tray**

OUR SALAD SELECTION CHANGES EVERY DAY

TAKE-OUT SALAD BOXES

SARA JANE, OUR PASTRY CHEF

PASTRY

Why is it that the combination of simple basic ingredients –
flour, butter, salt, egg yolk and water – can give such varied
results? There must be many reasons, but the main ones are:

* The quality of the butter and flour: first make sure the butter
is good quality and unsalted – Normandy butter if possible;
second, the flour must not be a fine cake flour but something
stronger, approaching a bread flour – we use a traditional
French flour, which is perfect.
* The temperature of your hands – they have to be cool.
* The weather – the hotter the day, the less water you will need.
* Speed of execution – the less you handle the dough, the
lighter the pastry will be. At Rose Bakery we use a food
processor to work the flour, salt and butter together, which
means you handle the dough much less and it is much
quicker, but this is not essential – you can do it by hand.
* How you bring the dough together – again, the more
quickly, the better.

MAKING SHORTCRUST PASTRY

SHORTCRUST PASTRY

This pastry dough can be frozen if you don't want to make three large tarts at once, but it is best to roll it out into tins before freezing as it can be difficult to deal with otherwise. Just freeze the pastry in the tart tins, uncooked and wrapped in cling film (plastic wrap). You can then bake from frozen when needed – unwrap the tins and place them directly in the preheated oven.

Enough to make 3 x 28 cm (11 inch) **tart cases** (crusts)
500 g (3⅓ cups) **plain** (all-purpose) **flour**
½ teaspoon salt
250 g (generous 1 cup) **cold unsalted butter, plus extra for greasing**
1 egg yolk
about 250 ml (1 cup) **cold water**

If you are using a food processor, process the flour, salt and butter for about 5–8 seconds, so that some pieces of butter are left, then put the mixture in a bowl. Otherwise, put the flour and salt in a bowl, cut the butter into pieces and work it into the flour with your fingertips.

Now make a well in the middle of the flour and butter mixture and add the egg yolk and half the water (only a third on a very hot day – it's only in the coldest months that we use up all the water). Stir quickly with a fork to start bringing the dry and wet ingredients together, adding more water if needed.

When the fork can't do any more, use your hands just to bring the dough together. There is no kneading or pressing – all you have to do is gather up the dry parts as quickly as possible. Make sure you don't have a sticky mess or a dry crumbly mound. If your hands get too warm put them under cold water for few minutes.

Wrap the dough in cling film and chill in the fridge for at least 30 minutes – or up to 8 hours.

Variations
I sometimes add the following to the flour:
* **A handful of wholemeal** (wholewheat) **flour**
* **About 2 large handfuls** (1 cup) **chopped chives**
* **A pinch of cayenne pepper and 50 g** (½ cup) **grated Cheddar cheese**
* **A pinch of ground cinnamon, especially for an onion pissaladière (see page 93)**
* **40 g** (¼ cup) **polenta flour or semolina for a crunchy texture**

VEGETABLE TARTS

VEGETABLE TARTS

Our little tarts and quiches, the square moulds for which
we had specially made in France, are without doubt the
most popular item on the counter at lunchtime – we can
never make enough. A huge effort goes into filling them
each day, with so many variations and combinations of
vegetables, herbs and meats. This selection is really a
very simplified version of what we actually do! So you
must feel free to experiment too, using our recipes for
the cream mixture and its casing as guidelines.

TART CASE (CRUST)

Preheat the oven to 180°C/350°F/Gas Mark 4
and grease 3 x 28 cm (11 inch) tart tins (quiche
pans) with butter.

Take the dough out of the fridge and divide it
into three pieces.

Dust your work surface and rolling pin with lots
of flour and roll out one of the pieces, lifting and
turning it all the time so that it does not stick
to the surface.

When it reaches a thickness of about
4 mm (⅛ inch) – less if possible – use it to line
a tart tin. Make sure you don't stretch the
dough to make it fit. Just ease it in with
a little extra to spare – this will stop the
pastry shrinking.

Repeat the process with the remaining pieces
of dough.

Chill again for about 30 minutes.

Bake the tart cases blind with any weight
system you have (we use foil filled with beans)
for about 25–30 minutes. The pastry must be
dry and just turning golden.

Cool for a while.

CREAM MIXTURE

Enough for 1 x 28 cm (11 inch) tart
500 ml (2 cups) single (light) cream
4 eggs
1 egg yolk
pinch each of salt and ground black pepper
pinch of grated nutmeg

Beat all the ingredients together in a bowl
until they are well mixed.

FILLINGS

There is a huge variety of fillings for vegetable
tarts, all of which involve adding different
ingredients to the basic cream mixture.
Here are some suggestions:
* 8 rashers (slices) of bacon, grated Cheddar
cheese and 2 tomatoes, sliced
* 4–5 slices of smoked salmon and fresh dill
(no cheese)
* 6–8 roasted courgettes (zucchini) and 2 red
peppers (bell peppers)
* 1 medium to large butternut squash, roasted
and puréed, with only a quarter of the cream
mixture, topped with pine nuts.

PREPARING VEGETABLE TARTS

MUSHROOM AND CHIVE TART

Serves 6–8
2 tablespoons extra virgin olive oil
400 g (5 cups) **mushrooms, sliced**
1 garlic clove, crushed
salt and ground black pepper
200 g (2 cups) **grated Cheddar cheese**
1 x 28 cm (11 inch) **Tart Case (see page 89)**
1 quantity Cream Mixture (see page 89)
1 handful chopped chives

Preheat the oven to 180°C/350°F/Gas Mark 4.

Heat the oil in a frying pan and fry the mushrooms with the garlic and salt and pepper till all the liquid has gone.

Scatter the cheese over the base of the tart case. Place the mushrooms on this and pour in as much of the cream mixture as you can without it spilling over the top.

Sprinkle with the chives and transfer carefully to the oven.

Bake for about 30 minutes till the filling has set and is lightly golden.

ARTICHOKE AND PEA TART

Serves 6–8
8 globe artichokes
salt and ground black pepper
150 g (1½ cups) **grated Parmesan cheese**
1 x 28 cm (11 inch) **Tart Case (see page 89)**
250 g (2½ cups) **peas, cooked, or thawed if frozen**
½ quantity Cream Mixture (see page 89)
1 large handful chopped fresh mint
110 g (½ cup) **ricotta cheese**
grated zest of 1 lemon

First prepare the artichokes. Remove the stalks and the tips of the outer leaves, and cook the artichokes in salted boiling water for about 30 minutes.

Remove the tough outer leaves and the chokes and cut the artichokes into slices.

Preheat the oven to 180°C/350°F/Gas Mark 4.

Scatter the Parmesan over the base of the tart case, and cover with the artichoke slices.

Put the peas and cream mixture into a food processor and liquidize with the mint, ricotta and lemon zest.

Pour over the artichokes.

Transfer carefully to the oven and bake for about 30 minutes or until the filling has set and is lightly golden.

READY FOR THE OVEN

RICOTTA, TOMATO AND THYME TART

Serves 6–8
6 tomatoes, halved
salt and ground black pepper
extra virgin olive oil, for drizzling
100 g (1 cup) **grated Cheddar cheese**
1 x 28 cm (11 inch) **Tart Case (see page 89)**
350 g (1½ cups) **ricotta cheese**
1 quantity Cream Mixture (see page 89)
1 handful chopped fresh thyme

Preheat the oven to 180°C/350°F/Gas Mark 4.

Bake the tomatoes skin-side up for about 45 minutes, until the liquid has gone and the skins can easily be removed.

Season the tomatoes with salt and pepper and drizzle a little oil over them.

Scatter the Cheddar cheese over the base of the tart case. Place the tomatoes on top of this and spoonfuls of ricotta over the tomatoes.

Pour in as much of the cream mixture as you can without it spilling over the top. Sprinkle with the thyme.

Transfer carefully to the oven and bake for about 30 minutes till the filling has set and is lightly golden.

ONION PISSALADIÈRE

Unlike the other vegetable tarts, the pissaladière does not contain any cream mixture.

Serves 6–8
4 tablespoons extra virgin olive oil
10–12 onions, sliced
1 garlic clove, crushed
pinch of ground cinnamon
1 teaspoon sugar
1 x 28 cm (11 inch) **Tart Case (see page 89)**
3 medium tomatoes, sliced
1 handful black olives
salt and ground black pepper

Preheat the oven to 180°C/350°F/Gas Mark 4.

Put the oil in a heavy-based saucepan and add the onions and garlic. Season with salt and pepper. Cook over a very low heat, stirring occasionally, till the onions are completely soft.

Add the sugar and cinnamon to the softened onions.

Fill the case with the softened onions, then top with the tomatoes and olives, and season to taste.

Transfer carefully to the oven and bake for about 10–15 minutes.

PIZZETTE

PIZZETTE

Like the vegetable tarts, our pizette sell out within the hour at lunchtime. And, as with the tarts, the toppings vary according to what's in season and available, so it all comes down to selecting your favourite combinations, whether it's tomatoes and rocket (arugula) or onions, courgettes (zucchini) and mozarella, and so on.

PIZZETTE DOUGH

The recipe calls for the dough for the pizzette to be left to rise overnight, but if you want to avoid this step you can leave the dough to double in size in a warm place for about 1½ hours.

Makes about 14 pizzette
500 g (3⅓ cups) **strong white flour** (bread flour), preferably unbleached, plus extra for dusting
1 handful **wholemeal** (wholewheat) **flour**
20 g (¾ oz) **fresh yeast**
½ teaspoon **brown sugar**
50 ml (¼ cup) **extra virgin olive oil**, plus extra for greasing
2 teaspoons **salt**
about 80 g (½ cup) **semolina**

The day before you want to make the pizzette, put both flours into a bowl. Make a well in the middle, crumble in the yeast and add the sugar and 100 ml (scant ½ cup) **hand-warm water.**

Mix a little of the flour into the yeast-and-water mixture and leave to rest for about 15 minutes.

When the mixture begins to bubble, add the oil, salt and 200 ml (scant 1 cup) **hand-warm water** to the bowl. Mix well, then turn out on a lightly floured surface.

Knead the dough for about 10 minutes till it is smooth and soft but not sticky. Add more flour if necessary.

Place in an oiled bowl, cover with cling film (plastic wrap) **and place in the fridge overnight.**

The following day, take the dough out of the fridge and let it rise further for about 1 hour.

Preheat the oven to 200°C/400°F/Gas Mark 6.

Punch the dough down and divide it into about 14 pieces. Dust the work surface with a mixture of flour and semolina and roll the pieces out to make 10–12 cm (4–5 inch) **circles.**

If you have trouble making the circles look nice, take them in your hands and keep turning them, holding the edges, till you get decent shapes. Don't worry if they are not perfect. This is rustic food after all.

Brush a baking tray (or trays) with oil. Spread your chosen topping ingredients over the circles and place the pizzette on the baking tray.

Bake for about 10–15 minutes.

PIZZETTE TOPPINGS

We make two pizzette-base mixtures:
* Finely diced tomatoes (when they are in season and full-flavoured) with olive oil, salt, pepper, garlic and fresh oregano or basil.
* Thinly sliced onions stewed in olive oil, with salt, pepper, garlic and thyme or oregano.

Both mixtures are moist. Spread them lightly over the pizzette leaving a 1 cm (½ inch) margin around the edges.

You can put any vegetables you like on top of the pizzette, but keep it simple. Some of our favourite combinations are:
* **Sliced roasted courgettes** (zucchini), **a couple of halved cherry tomatoes and a dollop of ricotta cheese.**
* **Sliced artichokes, Parmesan cheese shavings and lots of chopped fresh parsley.**
* **Extra tomatoes added to the tomato base and, when they are cooked, a handful of rocket** (arugula) **leaves, a drizzle of olive oil and a pinch of Maldon sea salt** (or Kosher salt).

RISOTTO

I think I could practically live on risotto, carrots and apricots. There is something truly wonderful about a perfect bowl of risotto, made correctly, full of flavour, slightly «al dente» and almost like a soup. There is always a risotto on the menu, first because I love it, but also because, although there is an abundance of pasta and Italian places in Paris, I have yet to taste a good risotto at any of them! Again the choice is endless, but here are a few recipes. You can replace my suggestions with any of your favourite vegetables to make a delicious risotto. The day the photograph opposite was taken, we had made a porcini and tomato risotto at Rose Bakery, so that is what you see here. My very special one is softened leeks with chestnuts! You can even use seafood with a fish stock (I don't add Parmesan cheese to fish risottos which means they have to be seasoned very carefully).

TOMATO, AUBERGINE (EGGPLANT) AND MINT RISOTTO

Serves 6
8 tomatoes, halved
3 aubergines (eggplants)**, cut into 3 cm** (1¼ inch) **chunks**
4 tablespoons extra virgin olive oil, plus extra for roasting the vegetables
60 g (¼ cup) **unsalted butter**
2 onions, finely diced
salt and ground black pepper
400 g (generous 1¾ cups) **carnaroli rice**
1½ litres (6 cups) **hot vegetable or chicken stock**
100 g (1 cup) **grated Parmesan cheese**
2 large handfuls chopped fresh mint
1 teaspoon caster (superfine) **sugar (optional)**
grated Parmesan cheese or chopped fresh mint, to garnish

Preheat the oven to 200°C/400°F/Gas Mark 6.

First roast the tomatoes skin-side up for about 30 minutes, until the liquid has gone and the skins can easily be removed. Roast the aubergine chunks, well covered with oil, alongside the tomatoes for the same length of time until they are soft but not rubbery.

Put 4 tablespoons oil and the butter in a heavy-based saucepan and add the onions and a pinch of salt. Cook over a very low heat, stirring occasionally, till the onions are soft but have not yet started to brown.

Pour in the rice and cook over a medium heat, stirring, till it becomes translucent.

Pour in the stock a ladleful at a time and cook, stirring, until the rice has absorbed all the liquid before adding more.

After about 5 minutes, add the roasted tomatoes and aubergines.

Carry on adding the stock until you have a very creamy consistency. The rice must be cooked but slightly 'al dente', and the mixture must hold together.

Remove from the heat and add the Parmesan and mint.

Stir well and check the seasoning. Because of the acid in the tomatoes you may need to add a little sugar.

Pour the risotto into bowls and garnish with a little more Parmesan or mint, as desired.

COURGETTE (ZUCCHINI) AND MILLET RISOTTO

Serves 6
500 g (1 pound 2 ounces) **courgettes** (zucchini)
5 tablespoons extra virgin olive oil, plus extra for coating
salt and ground black pepper
150 g (¾ cup) **millet**
60 g (¼ cup) **unsalted butter**
2 onions, finely sliced
1 garlic clove, crushed
400 g (generous 1¾ cups) **carnaroli rice**
about 1½ litres (6 cups) **vegetable or chicken stock (this is better hot but not necessary)**
100–150 g (1–1½ cups) **grated Parmesan cheese**
grated Parmesan cheese or chopped fresh parsley, to garnish

Preheat the oven to 200°C/400°F/Gas Mark 6.

First roast the courgettes. Cut into medium slices, approximately 5 mm (¼ inch) thick, and spread out evenly on a baking tray. Drizzle a little olive oil over the sliced courgettes, season with salt and pepper and roast for about 30 minutes until golden. Set aside.

Prepare the millet next as this grain cooks at a different pace from the rice and it's best to have it ready. Put it into a heavy-based saucepan and toast it over a high heat, stirring constantly, for 3–5 minutes until it smells fragrant and nutty.

Pour on 475 ml (1¾ cups) boiling water, add 1 tablespoon of the oil and a little salt and simmer, covered, for about 20 minutes until all the liquid has been absorbed. If the grains are still too crunchy put a lid on the saucepan, turn off the heat and leave the millet to cook in its own steam for a further 10 minutes. Fluff up and leave aside.

Put the remaining 4 tablespoons oil and the butter in another heavy-based saucepan and add the onions and a pinch each of salt and pepper. Cook over a very low heat, stirring occasionally, till the onions are soft but have not yet started to brown.

Add the garlic and stir for a few minutes.

Pour in the rice and cook over a medium heat, stirring, till it becomes translucent.

Pour in the stock a ladleful at a time and cook, stirring, until the rice has absorbed all the liquid before adding some more. After about 5 minutes, add the courgette slices.

Carry on adding the stock until you have a very creamy consistency. The rice must be cooked but slightly 'al dente', and the mixture must hold together.

Remove from the heat and add Parmesan to taste.

Stir well and check the seasoning. However good the stock, until this point you never know what the risotto needs.

Pour the risotto into bowls and garnish with a little more Parmesan, or parsley, as desired.

MUSHROOM AND PORCINI RISOTTO

This is a classic, and no selection of risotto recipes would seem right without the inclusion of one using flavourful porcini, which are also knows as ceps.

Serves 6
1 handful dried porcini, soaked in 400 ml
  (1¾ cups) **hot water for about 30 minutes**
4 tablespoons olive oil, plus extra for frying
500 g (7¼ cups) **mushrooms, sliced**
1 garlic clove, crushed
salt and ground black pepper
60 g (¼ cup) **unsalted butter**
2 onions, finely diced
400 g (generous 1¾ cups) **carnaroli rice**
about 1½ litres (6 cups) **vegetable or**
  chicken stock
150 g (1½ cups) **grated Parmesan cheese**

Strain the porcini and reserve their soaking liquid. Set both aside.

Heat a generous amount of oil in a frying pan and fry the mushrooms with the garlic and salt and pepper. Set aside.

Put 4 tablespoons oil and the butter in a heavy-based saucepan and add the onions and a pinch of salt. Cook over a very low heat, stirring occasionally, till the onions are soft but have not yet started to brown.

Pour in the rice and cook over a medium heat, stirring, till it becomes translucent.

Add the porcini and some of their liquid and the sliced mushrooms.

Pour in the stock a ladleful at a time and cook, stirring, until the rice has absorbed all the liquid before adding some more. Carry on adding the stock until you have a very creamy consistency. The rice must be cooked but slightly 'al dente', and the mixture must hold together.

Remove from the heat and add the Parmesan.

Stir well and check the seasoning.

Pour the risotto into bowls and serve immediately.

COD IN TOMATO WATER

At Rose Bakery we have one or two main courses on the menu every day, as well as a risotto. Whether it is chicken, beef, lamb or fish, a dish is always inspired by the vegetables that are available. For instance, making a fresh tomato broth comes before deciding to poach fish in it. If a crate of globe artichokes is just in, our first thought is to braise them, and then we might possibly decide to accompany them with lamb or chicken. Our favourite way of cooking has to be braising, so we cook a lot of stews. Again, we start with the vegetables we have, whether it's a selection of fresh summer choices, or, in winter, leeks, potatoes and root vegetables. Each main course is a vegetable dish, accompanied by meat.

COD IN TOMATO WATER

Enormous ethical issues are associated with cod and many other white fish that we have enjoyed eating over the years. If you decide to use cod, perhaps you could try to find blue cod from New Zealand or Icelandic cod, which is a more sustainable source, from seas where this fish is protected and sources are carefully controlled. Other kinds of fish for this recipe could be hake, sea bass or turbot, but they are also under threat, so the decision is ultimately yours.

Serves 4
4 cod fillets

For the tomato water
4 tablespoons olive oil
2 large handfuls chopped fresh flat-leaf parsley
3 garlic cloves, crushed
pinch of dried red Thai chilli (chile)
1 teaspoon salt
4 medium tomatoes, peeled and chopped
1 tablespoon tomato purée (paste)

To garnish
chopped fresh flat-leaf parsley
olive oil, for drizzling

To make the tomato water, place all the ingredients in a wide saucepan with 1 litre (4 cups) water and simmer, uncovered, for about 30 minutes till reduced by a third.

Gently place the cod fillets in the liquid and poach for about 5 minutes until just cooked. Remove the fish and put in serving bowls.

Turn the heat to high and reduce the tomato water by half.

Pour over the fish (you can strain it first if you prefer) and top each serving with extra parsley and a drizzle of olive oil.

BRAISED ARTICHOKE, LEMON AND LAMB CHOPS

BRAISED ARTICHOKE, LEMON AND LAMB CHOPS

Serves 6
juice of 2 lemons (for acidulated water)
12–14 medium globe artichokes
4 tablespoons extra virgin olive oil, plus extra
  for frying the chops
3 onions, finely diced
1 celery heart (the inner yellow part), finely
  sliced
3 carrots, finely diced
1 teaspoon salt
pinch of ground black pepper
grated zest of 1 lemon
2 garlic cloves, crushed
about 750 ml (3 cups) vegetable or chicken stock
  or water
1 teaspoon caster (superfine) sugar (optional)
18 lamb chops
chopped fresh flat-leaf parsley, to garnish

Half-fill a large bowl with water and add the
lemon juice.

To prepare the artichokes, remove their stalks
and the tips of their outer leaves, then peel
them down to the pale leaves. Halve them
downwards and scoop out and discard
the chokes.

Put the artichokes in the acidulated water
to stop them turning brown.

Heat 4 tablespoons oil in a saucepan and
cook the onions over a low heat until softened.

Add the celery, carrots, salt, pepper and
lemon zest. Continue to cook over a low heat
until all the vegetables are just turning golden –
about 15 minutes.

Add the garlic and the artichoke hearts.

Pour in enough stock or water to cover the
vegetables and simmer for about 15–20 minutes
until the artichokes are just cooked, and the
liquid has reduced by half.

Check the seasoning and add the sugar if the
vegetables are too sour. Set aside.

Season the chops and fry them in oil, or grill
them, till they are cooked through but still
slightly pink inside – about 5 minutes each side.

Serve with the artichokes on the side or
underneath the chops.

Garnish with parsley.

ASPARAGUS AND ALMOND SALAD WITH CHICKEN

This salad can be served warm or cold. We like to serve the cooked but cold asparagus and almonds with hot chicken pieces – a mixture of hot and cold!

Serves 6
18 asparagus spears (green or white), trimmed
1 handful whole almonds, skinned
6 skinless boneless chicken breasts
extra virgin olive oil, for frying (optional)
salt and ground black pepper
rocket (arugula) leaves, to garnish

For the dresssing
2 shallots, finely diced
4 tablespoons red wine vinegar
2 large handfuls chopped fresh flat-leaf parsley
salt and ground black pepper
75 ml (⅓ cup) extra virgin olive oil

Preheat the oven to 180°C/350°F/Gas Mark 4.

Place the asparagus in simmering water and cook for about 5 minutes until the spears are just cooked – they must be a little 'al dente'. Drain and set aside to cool.

Meanwhile, place the almonds in a roasting pan, drizzle over a little olive oil and roast for about 15 minutes till they are lightly golden. Set aside to cool.

Fry the chicken breasts in oil, or grill them, till they are cooked through, and season well with salt and pepper. Set aside to cool.

Cut the asparagus spears into 3–4 cm (1¼–1½ inch) pieces.

Slice the chicken breasts diagonally into four or five pieces.

Make the dressing by combining all the ingredients in a large bowl and mixing well, adding the oil at the end.

Carefully fold the chicken, asparagus and almonds into the dressing.

Divide the salad between six plates and garnish each serving with a small handful of rocket leaves.

FISH BALLS IN BROTH

I have to thank my mother for this recipe, as she makes the best gefilte fish balls in the world. This recipe is not exactly hers, but is definitely inspired by it. You can serve the fish balls warm with blanched vegetables and a strong horseradish sauce, or cold with a green or potato salad and a strong horseradish and **beetroot** (beet) **sauce** (Jewish chrain).

Serves 4
1 tablespoon sunflower or rapeseed (canola) oil, plus extra for frying
1 onion, sliced
600 g (1 pound 3 ounces) **white fish fillets (cod, haddock, brill, etc.), checked for bones and cut into about 4 cm** (1½ inch) **pieces**
1 egg
1 teaspoon salt
pinch of ground black pepper
1 teaspoon sugar
1 carrot, blanched and chopped
40 g (¼ cup) **fresh breadcrumbs**
2 tablespoons ground almonds

For the broth
2 onions, roughly chopped
2 sticks celery, chopped
1 carrot, chopped
2 bay leaves
1 teaspoon salt
pinch of ground black pepper
pinch of ground cinnamon

Put all the ingredients for the broth in a saucepan with **1½ litres** (6 cups) **water** and bring to the boil, then turn the heat down and simmer for 30 minutes.

Meanwhile, make the fish balls. Heat a little oil in a frying pan and fry the onion until softened.

Put the fish, egg, salt, pepper, sugar, onion, carrot, breadcrumbs, ground almonds and 1 tablespoon oil in a food processor and process until well mixed, but do not overmix. If the mixture is too wet add more ground almonds or breadcrumbs.

Check the seasoning.

Divide the mixture into golf-ball-sized balls and gently slip them into the broth.

Poach for about 15–20 minutes until cooked.

SALMON FILLETS AND BROCCOLI

The salmon we use comes from the west coast of Ireland and is organic. This recipe is inspired by the Japanese restaurants we often go to and I think it is one of the nicest ways to eat salmon, which is a very rich fish. You will need a wide, shallow pan with a heavy base. And make sure it is ovenproof – the salmon is cooked in the oven as well as on the hob (stovetop).

Serves 4
12 broccoli florets
sesame oil, for frying
4 salmon fillets
toasted sesame seeds, to garnish

For the sauce
120 ml (½ cup) **shoyu (soy sauce)**
1 garlic clove, finely chopped
1 dried red chilli (chile)
5 mm (¼ inch) **piece of fresh ginger, finely chopped**
2 tablespoons caster (superfine) sugar
1 tablespoon sesame oil

Preheat the oven to 190°C/375°F/Gas Mark 5.

Put all the ingredients for the sauce into a saucepan with **50 ml** (¼ cup) **water** and bring to the boil, then turn the heat down and simmer for about 15 minutes till slightly reduced. Set aside.

Meanwhile, blanch the broccoli florets till they are 'al dente'.

Now cook the salmon. Heat a little sesame oil in a pan and put the salmon fillets in, flesh-side down. Cook for about 5 minutes till golden. Turn the fillets over and put them in the oven till they are just cooked through – another 5 minutes.

Take them out of the pan and keep them warm.

Strain the sauce, pour it into the pan and boil over a medium heat until it has reduced – it needs to be thick enough to glaze the fish – and is nearly caramelized.

To serve, place the fillets on individual plates, skin-side down, with the broccoli florets on the side and the sauce poured over the fish. Sprinkle with sesame seeds and serve immediately.

BRAISED LAMB SHANKS WITH CUMIN,
AUBERGINES AND CHICKPEAS

BRAISED LAMB SHANKS WITH CUMIN, AUBERGINES (EGGPLANTS) AND CHICKPEAS (GARBANZO BEANS)

Serves 6
about 50 g (scant ¼ cup) **unsalted butter**
6 lamb shanks, neatly trimmed of all fat
4 tablespoons extra virgin olive oil, plus extra
   for roasting the aubergines (eggplants)
2 medium onions, roughly chopped
3 sticks celery, roughly chopped
3 carrots, roughly chopped
1 dried red chilli (chile)**, crushed**
5 garlic cloves, crushed
3 tablespoons ground cumin
2 tablespoons honey
1 tablespoon tomato purée (paste)
750 ml (3 cups) **vegetable or chicken stock**
   or water
4 aubergines (eggplants)**, cut into large chunks**
pinch of ground cinnamon (optional)
500 g (1 pound 2 ounces) **cooked chickpeas**
   (garbanzo beans)
salt and ground black pepper
chopped fresh coriander or mint, to garnish
   (optional)

Preheat the oven to 160°C/325°F/Gas Mark 3.

Heat the butter in an ovenproof pan large enough to take all the lamb shanks and seal the shanks well. Set them aside.

Add the oil, all the vegetables, the chilli and the garlic, and 1 teaspoon salt to help release the flavours, and cook over a medium to high heat till the vegetables begin to turn golden – about 15 minutes. Add the cumin and stir for 4 minutes.

Return the shanks to the dish, add the honey and tomato purée and cover with the stock or water.

Bring to the boil, skim the surface, cover and transfer to the oven.

Cook for about 1½ hours until the meat is very tender. Keep checking to see that the liquid is bubbling very slowly.

Towards the end of the cooking time place the aubergines in a roasting pan, splash them generously with oil and season with salt and pepper.

When the shanks are wonderfully tender take them out the oven and carefully remove them to a warm baking dish with a lid. Strain the liquid into a saucepan.

Raise the oven temperature to 220°C/425°F/Gas Mark 7, place the aubergines in the oven and roast them for about 30 minutes till they are golden and soft.

Meanwhile, over a high heat, reduce the liquid from the shanks by half, skimming often to remove any excess fat.

Taste for seasoning, and add more salt, pepper or honey if needed. I sometimes add a pinch of cinnamon at this stage.

Add the chickpeas, warm them through and pour them over the shanks.

Carefully place the hot, roasted aubergines around the shanks, cover and reheat the whole dish for about 30 minutes.

Garnish with coriander and mint, if you wish.

TEA

TARTS

SWEET PASTRY/SWEET TART CASE
LEMON TART
LEMON BLUEBERRY TART
CARAMEL PRALINE TART
CHESTNUT AND CHOCOLATE TARTLET
APRICOT AND ALMOND TART
CHOCOLATE, ORANGE AND RICOTTA TART
APPLE, NUT AND SPICE TORTE
PECAN PIE
RHUBARB MERINGUE TARTLETS

CAKES

CARROT CAKE
LEMON CAKE
BANANA CAKE
ORANGE ALMOND CAKES
FRESH GINGER CAKE
LEMON, RICE AND POLENTA CAKE
FRUIT CAKE (CHRISTMAS CAKE)
VEGAN FRUIT CAKE
PISTACHIO CAKE
RICOTTA CHEESECAKE
ARTICHOKE AND TOMATO CAKE
BROCCOLI CAKE

BISCUITS AND COOKIES

PECAN BISCUITS
SHORTBREAD
ALMOND CINNAMON AND MERINGUE BISCUITS
HOT GINGERNUT BISCUITS
CHOCOLATE CHIP BISCUITS
PEANUT BUTTER AND CHOCOLATE
CHIP BISCUITS
ROLLED FRUIT COOKIES
PINE NUT AND ALMOND BISCUITS
GINGERBREAD BISCUITS
OAT AND COCONUT COOKIES
JAM SANDWICH VEGAN COOKIES
ECCLES CAKES

TRAY BAKES

DATE AND OAT SLICES
COCONUT CUSTARD SLICES
HAZELNUT BROWNIES
BROWNIE CHEESECAKE
APRICOT, ALMOND AND RICOTTA SLICES
RED BEAN SLICES

PUDDINGS

APPLE AND BLACKBERRY CRUMBLE
OAT AND APPLE BETTY
APPLE BROWN BETTY
RICE PUDDING/RIZ AU LAIT
TOFFEE PUDDINGS
RICE, COCONUT AND TROPICAL
FRUIT CAKES
OUR CLASSIC CHOCOLATE MOUSSE
CARAMEL ICE CREAM
SUMMER PUDDING
ETON MESS
APRICOT SORBET
RED BEAN SORBET

SWEET TEA-TIME

I could drink tea and eat cake all day, any time of the day.
I don't have the time, thank goodness, but for me cake-and-
tea moments are some of the loveliest and simplest of
pleasures, and our customers feel the same. At first there
was a lot of hesitancy on the part of Parisians when it came
to carrot cake or date and oat slices. Carrots in a cake?
Oats? – never! But after the first bite there was no turning
back, and what is really wonderful now is that when there
is something new on the counter or menu, we are told:
«I don't know what that is, but I trust you and I'm sure it
is delicious.» This makes me smile with such feelings of
satisfaction, gratitude and relief. Perhaps there is no room
for emotion in a cookery book, but baking a good cake or
biscuits, or making a pudding and placing it, still warm,
on the counter is all to do with pleasure and making people
happy. Why else bother? Although many of the following
recipes are more suitable for tea, we tend to sell them as
desserts – a cookie with coffee, a slice of cheesecake or
lemon tart. As we are especially busy at lunchtimes,
this is only natural.

TARTS

As you will see in the following recipes, the basic principles
for making sweet tarts are very simple. The case or crust is
almost always made with sweet pastry, although I may use
a savoury one for some tarts – apple ones, for example –
for a less sweet overall flavour. The cases are almost always
prebaked to keep them crisp and the fillings are simple.

THE COUNTER AT TEA-TIME

SWEET PASTRY

Unlike savoury pastry ('pâte brisée') which hates being handled at all, sweet pastry loves to be worked – not as much as bread, but worked nonetheless. So with the understanding that it is completely different from savoury pastry, and is not just savoury pastry with added sugar, you can approach it differently. This recipe is based on the Italian sweet pastry 'pasta frolla', rather than the fine French 'pâte sucrée'. It is less fragile than the French one and can be rolled immediately it is made, without the normal rest period. In fact, if you do chill it for a while in the fridge it becomes very difficult to work with. Any unused pastry must be rolled and placed in tins straight away, and then frozen in the tins, uncooked and wrapped in cling film (plastic wrap). The quantities can be halved for smaller tarts.

Enough for 2 x 28 cm (11 inch) **tart cases** (crusts)
500 g (3⅓ cups) **plain** (all-purpose) **flour**
   (cake flour is fine)
120 g (generous ⅔ cup) **caster** (superfine) **sugar**
320 g (scant 1½ cups) **unsalted butter (10 minutes**
   out of the fridge), plus extra for greasing
pinch of salt
1 egg
2 egg yolks
1 teaspoon natural vanilla extract

If you are using a food processor, process the flour, sugar, butter and salt for about 10–12 seconds until the mixture resembles fine breadcrumbs, then put the mixture in a bowl. Otherwise, put the flour, sugar and salt in a bowl, cut the butter into pieces and work it into the flour with your fingertips.

Now make a well in the middle of the flour-and-butter mixture and add the egg, egg yolks and vanilla extract. Stir with a fork to incorporate the flour evenly until you have to begin using your hand.

Using one hand only, bring the dry and wet ingredients together (this might take more time in winter).

Dust your work surface with flour, then remove the dough from the bowl and knead it on the floured surface for a few minutes until it is smooth and homogeneous.

It is now ready to be rolled.

SWEET TART CASE (CRUST)

Preheat the oven to 180°C/350°F/Gas Mark 4 and grease 2 x 28 cm (11 inch) tart tins with butter.

Prepare the dough (see left), then cut it in two. Wrap one half in cling film (plastic wrap) and either set it aside in winter, or put it briefly in the fridge if it is a hot day.

Flour your work surface well, then roll out the dough to a thickness of about 5 mm (¼ inch).

Carefully lift it up with the rolling pin, as it does tend to break, and ease it into the tart tin. If it does break, don't worry – just patch it up with extra dough.

Repeat the process with the remaining dough.

Now you have to chill the tart cases for at least 30 minutes before baking, or you can freeze them if you wish to use them later.

Bake blind with any weight system you have (we use foil filled with beans) for about 20 minutes until the pastry is just turning golden.

Leave to cool before filling.

TARTLETS

For individual tartlets, cut smaller pieces of dough and roll enough to fill your size tin. Just ease it in and cut off the excess bits.

Re-use any extra bits in the next piece of dough and so on.

AFTER THE RUSH IN OUR PASTRY KITCHEN

LEMON TART

Our lemon tart is actually a double lemon tart, as it consists of two mixtures. This came about because the classic lemon filling often cracked and ruined the appearance of the tart. So we decided to cover the top, once cooked, with a simple lemon curd, which gives a lovely, perfect and stable topping. **We find it is best to prepare the curd the day before we use it and chill it overnight in the fridge. We also use a slightly deeper tart tin, about 3 cm (1¼ inches), to take all the filling. You can halve the quantities in the recipe if you want a smaller tart.**

Serves 8
1 prebaked 28 cm (11 inch) **Sweet Tart Case**
  (see page 114), glazed with beaten egg
220 ml (scant 1 cup) **lemon juice**
165 g (generous ¾ cup) **caster** (superfine) **sugar**
8 eggs
2 egg yolks
70 ml (⅓ cup) **single** (light) **cream**
1 tablespoon plain (all-purpose) **flour**

For the lemon curd
2 eggs
5 egg yolks
110 g (generous ½ cup) **caster** (superfine) **sugar**
110 ml (scant ½ cup) **lemon juice**
60 g (¼ cup) **unsalted butter**

Preheat the oven to **180°C / 350°F / Gas Mark 4** and bake the tart case for 5 minutes. Remove and keep the oven switched on.

In a bowl, whisk the lemon juice with the sugar until well mixed, then beat in the eggs and egg yolks, one at a time.

Add the cream and whisk well, then whisk in the flour.

Strain the mixture into the tart case and bake for about 30 minutes or until the lemon cream is just set, with no bubbles or puffing up. Take out and leave to cool.

To make the lemon curd, put the eggs, egg yolks, sugar and lemon juice in a bowl set over a saucepan of simmering water. Stir constantly until the curd thickens, becomes smooth and keeps its shape when stirred.

Remove from the heat and stir in the butter.

Strain into a bowl and cover.

Chill in the fridge, overnight if possible, then spread it over the lemon cream as smoothly as you can.

This tart, like most of our tarts, is best eaten on the same day. If you want to keep it for the next day store it in the fridge.

LEMON BLUEBERRY TART

This is the same as the Lemon Tart (see left) except that, instead of the lemon curd, we spread a fresh blueberry mixture over the lemon cream.

Serves 8
1 prebaked 28 cm (11 inch) **Sweet Tart Case**
  (see page 114), glazed with beaten egg
220 ml (scant 1 cup) **lemon juice**
165 g (generous ¾ cup) **caster** (superfine) **sugar**
8 eggs
2 egg yolks
70 ml (⅓ cup) **single** (light) **cream**
1 tablespoon plain (all-purpose) **flour**

For the blueberry mixture
175 g (½ cup) **cherry, raspberry or strawberry jam**
3 punnets or 450 g (4 cups) **blueberries**

Preheat the oven to **180°C / 350°F / Gas Mark 4** and bake the tart case for 5 minutes. Remove and keep the oven switched on.

In a bowl, whisk the lemon juice with the sugar until well mixed, then beat in the eggs and egg yolks, one at a time.

Add the cream and whisk well, then whisk in the flour.

Strain the mixture into the tart case and bake for about 30 minutes or until the lemon cream is just set, with no bubbles or puffing up. Take out and leave to cool.

To make the blueberry mixture, put the jam in a saucepan and stir over a medium heat until bubbling.

Add the blueberries and continue stirring until they just begin to give off a darker colour – about 3–4 minutes.

Remove from the heat immediately, and pour over the lemon cream.

Each berry must be shiny and glazed.

SWEET TARTS

CARAMEL PRALINE TART

This is the tart for caramel fans and those
who hunger for sweet things.

Serves 8
1 prebaked 28 cm (11 inch) **Sweet Tart Case**
 (see page 114), glazed with beaten egg
220 g (generous 1 cup) **caster** (superfine) **sugar**
800 ml (scant 3¼ cups) **single** (light) **cream**
1 egg, beaten
6 egg yolks, beaten
crème fraîche (sour cream)**, to serve**

For the praline
unsalted butter, for greasing
220 g (generous 1 cup) **caster** (superfine) **sugar**
150 g (1¼ cups) **almonds, roughly chopped**

Preheat the oven to 160°C/325°F/Gas Mark 3
and bake the tart case for 5 minutes. Remove
and keep the oven switched on.

To make the praline, first grease a sheet
of parchment paper with butter.

Put the sugar in a saucepan with
85 ml (generous ⅓ cup) **water and cook over**
a low heat until the sugar has dissolved.
Then turn the heat to high and cook until
the liquid is a golden amber colour.

As soon as the colour is right remove from
the heat and add the almonds.

Put back on a low heat to liquefy the mixture
again, then pour the praline over the parchment
paper to cool.

When it is completely cold and hard, put it in a
food processor and grind it as fine as you want.
Or use a rolling pin to crush the praline between
two sheets of parchment paper. Set aside.

To make the filling, put the sugar in a large
saucepan with 85 ml (generous ⅓ cup) **water**
and cook over a low heat until the sugar has
dissolved. Then turn the heat to high and
cook until the liquid is a dark golden colour.

Meanwhile, heat the cream in another saucepan
until scalded.

Remove the caramel from the heat and place
the saucepan in the sink in case of spills.

Slowly pour in a little of the hot cream, taking
great care as it may bubble up furiously over
the top of the saucepan.

When things have calmed down, whisk in the
rest of the cream, and stir till well combined.

Set aside to cool, then whisk in the egg yolks
and egg and strain the mixture into the tart
case – fill it as high as possible.

Bake for about 25–30 minutes or until the filling
is just set. Do not bake it any longer as it will
begin to bubble and curdle.

Remove and set aside to cool.

When cooled, sprinkle the praline on top
and serve with crème fraîche.

PREPARING PRALINE

UNSALTED BUTTER IS BEST FOR BAKING

TEA-TIME ORDERS

CHESTNUT AND CHOCOLATE TARTLET

A surprising mix which works so well, especially if you love chestnuts as I do. The tartlets are great in winter. If you prefer, you can make one large tart in a 28 cm (11 inch) Sweet Tart Case (see page 114).

Serves 8
8 prebaked **Tartlet Cases** (see page 114), glazed with beaten egg
150 g (⅔ cup) **cream cheese**
500 g (1 pound 2 ounces) **sweetened chestnut purée**
2 eggs, beaten
1 teaspoon brandy or whisky

For the chocolate cream
180 g (6½ ounces) **roughly chopped dark (bittersweet) chocolate, at least 70% cocoa solids**
185 ml (scant ¾ cup) **single** (light) **cream**
1 egg yolk, beaten

Preheat the oven to 180°C/350°F/Gas Mark 4 and bake the tartlet cases for 5 minutes. Remove and keep the oven switched on.

In a bowl, mix together the cream cheese and chestnut purée.

Add the eggs and brandy or whisky.

Fill the tartlet cases with the mixture and bake until just set – about 25 minutes. Take out of the oven and set aside to cool.

Meanwhile, make the chocolate cream. Put the chocolate and cream in a saucepan and cook over a low heat, stirring, until the chocolate has melted.

Remove from the heat and immediately beat in the egg yolk.

When the tartlets have cooled, remove them from their tins and spread the chocolate cream over the chestnut filling.

APRICOT AND ALMOND TART

This has to be my favourite tart – once again because of the apricots. The combination of sweet and sour is perfect. Plums, peaches, poached pears, figs or apples are just as good if apricots are out of season.

Serves 8
1 prebaked 28 cm (11 inch) **Sweet Tart Case** (see page 114), glazed with beaten egg
250 g (generous 1 cup) **unsalted butter, softened**
250 g (1¼ cups) **caster** (superfine) **sugar**
2 eggs
2 egg yolks
1 teaspoon almond essence (optional)
250 g (2½ cups) **ground almonds**
50 g (⅓ cup) **plain** (all-purpose) **flour**

For the topping
500 g (1 pound 2 ounces) **apricots, halved and stoned**
4 tablespoons apricot jam
2 tablespoons lemon juice

Preheat the oven to 180°C/350°F/Gas Mark 4 and bake the tart case for 5 minutes. Remove and keep the oven switched on.

First make the almond filling, or frangipane. In a bowl, beat the butter well and add the sugar. Continue beating till the mixture is light and creamy.

Beat in the eggs and egg yolks, one at a time, with the almond essence.

Fold in the ground almonds and flour. The mixture should have a soft, cake-like consistency.

Spread the frangipane over the base of the tart case so that the case is about two-thirds full.

Starting on the outside edge, and continuing in circles till the filling is covered, place the apricots skin-side down on the frangipane. We tilt them upwards so that that they are almost standing up.

Bake for about 45 minutes till the apricots are tinged with brown and the frangipane is cooked and golden.

To make the topping, melt the jam in a saucepan with the lemon juice over a hight heat until it is bubbling squite strongly.

Brush the top of the apricots with the glaze to give them a nice shine.

CHOCOLATE, ORANGE AND RICOTTA TART

Like all cheesecake-type tarts this keeps well in the fridge for a few days, although it is always best served on the day it is made.

Serves 8
1 prebaked 28 cm (11 inch) **Sweet Tart Case (see page 114), glazed with beaten egg**
3 egg yolks
1 egg
100 g (½ cup) **caster** (superfine) **sugar**
1 teaspoon natural vanilla extract
grated zest of 2 oranges
500 g (scant 2¼ cups) **ricotta cheese**
100 ml (scant ½ cup) **single** (light) **cream**
120 g (4 ounces) **roughly chopped dark** (bittersweet) **chocolate, at least 70% cocoa solids**
1 tablespoon plain (all-purpose) **flour**

Preheat the oven to 180°C/350°F/Gas Mark 4 and bake the tart case for 5 minutes. Remove and keep the oven switched on.

Beat the egg yolks and egg with the sugar until light and fluffy. Add the vanilla extract, orange zest, ricotta and cream and mix well.

Fold the chocolate into the mixture and finally fold in the flour.

Pour into the tart case and bake for about 25–30 minutes until the filling has just set.

Remove from the oven, cool and serve at room temperature.

APPLE, NUT AND SPICE TORTE

Lots of our customers in Paris tell us that we have spelt this wrong – in French, it should be 'tarte'. So I have to keep explaining that this is an Italian tart, and because it has a top it is called a 'torte'! This is a good one for those who don't have a very sweet tooth.

Serves 8
500 g (1 pound 2 ounces) **Sweet Pastry (see page 114) for the top, and 1 uncooked 28 cm** (11 inch) **Sweet Tart Case (see page 114)**
plain (all-purpose) **flour, for dusting**
10 apples
1 teaspoon ground cinnamon
1 teaspoon ground mixed spice
100 g (½ cup) **caster** (superfine) **sugar**
grated zest of 1 lemon
120 g (1 cup) **roughly chopped almonds**
45 g (scant ½ cup) **ground almonds**
1 handful sultanas (golden raisins) **(optional)**
1 egg, beaten

Roll out the pastry for the top on a floured surface, to a thickness of 5 mm (¼ inch) and to the diameter of the tin being used. Chill this and the tart case in the fridge for 30 minutes.

Preheat the oven to 180°C/350°F/Gas Mark 4.

Grate the apples into a bowl (skin included if you wish). Squeeze out the extra juice to make the apples as dry as possible (wet apples will make the base soggy) and drink it!

Add the cinnamon, mixed spice and sugar to the apples.

Stir in the lemon zest and the chopped and ground almonds. You can also stir in the sultanas if you wish, but I prefer the 'torte' without them.

Brush the base and sides of the uncooked tart case with beaten egg, particularly the edges to make sure the top will be well sealed.

Spoon the apple mixture into the case, making sure it is raised and fills the case as the apples shrink a lot.

Carefully lift up the pastry for the top with a rolling pin and place it over the filling. Seal the edges well and cut a little hole in the middle to let out the steam.

Glaze the top with beaten egg and bake the 'torte' for about 1 hour till the pastry is golden and well cooked.

Cool on a wire rack and serve at room temperature.

PECAN PIE

This is an all-American speciality, but we are asked for it in England and in France too. Introducing maple syrup and reducing the sugar content makes it a perfect winter tart, when you are looking for something different from apples and pears to use as a filling.

Serves 8
1 prebaked 28 cm (11 inch) **Sweet Tart Case (see page 114), glazed with beaten egg**
300 g (2 cups) **pecan nuts**
4 large **eggs**
50 g (¼ cup) **caster** (superfine) **sugar**
250 ml (1 cup) **maple syrup**
90 g (generous ⅓ cup) **unsalted butter, melted**
crème fraîche (sour cream)**, to serve**

Preheat the oven to 180°C/350°F/Gas Mark 4 and bake the tart case for 5 minutes.

Place the pecans on a baking tray and roast them for about 20 minutes, stirring them once or twice. Remove and keep the oven switched on.

Roughly chop three-quarters of the pecans, and set the best ones aside for decoration.

In a bowl, beat together the eggs, sugar, maple syrup and butter.

Fold in the chopped pecans, mix well and pour into the tart case.

Decorate with the whole pecans and bake for about 25–30 minutes until just set.

Serve warm with crème fraîche.

RHUBARB MERINGUE TARTLETS

Rhubarb can be as sour as lemons, so one day we made this filling instead of the classic lemon meringue combination. It worked. But it works better as small individual tartlets.

Serves 8
8 prebaked **Tartlet Cases (see page 114), glazed with beaten egg**
5–6 sticks **rhubarb, cut into 6 cm** (2½ inch) **pieces**
200 g (1 cup) **caster** (superfine) **sugar**
grated zest of 1 orange

For the meringue
6 **egg whites**
350 g (1¾ cups) **caster** (superfine) **sugar**
1 teaspoon **natural vanilla extract**
1 teaspoon **red or white wine vinegar**
1 teaspoon **cream of tartar**

Preheat the oven to 180°C/350°F/Gas Mark 4 and bake the tartlet cases for 5 minutes. Remove and keep the oven switched on.

Place the rhubarb in a baking dish with the sugar and orange zest and cover with foil.

Bake for about 20 minutes until the rhubarb is soft and a good syrup has formed.

Remove from the oven and mix, mashing the rhubarb slightly. Set aside to cool. Keep the oven switched on.

To make the meringue, beat the egg whites till they form soft peaks, then slowly add the sugar. Beat constantly till the meringue is thick and glossy. Add the vanilla extract, vinegar and cream of tartar and fold in well.

Spoon the rhubarb mixture into the tartlet cases and pipe or spoon the meringue on top.

Bake for about 20–25 minutes until the meringue starts to turn brown and is slightly crisp.

AFTERNOON TEA

CAKES

As far back as I can remember my mother has made
cakes, so they have played a large part in my life – the
wonderful smell when they are freshly baked, the finger-
licking bowls of sweet raw batters, the flavours of vanilla
and lemon, chocolate and almond. I stopped eating them
as a teenager when, sadly, «weight issues» took over, but
the memories lingered, and when I started to make my
own cakes, recipes that used less sugar and «healthy»
cakes replaced my mother's sweet iced ones.

At Rose Bakery, we set out to offer healthier desserts
and cakes. Our recipes have therefore changed over time:
our chocolate cake, originally a signature dish, has been
usurped by our hazelnut brownie, muffins by scones.
We have reduced the sugar content in our renowned carrot
cake by half, but less sugar does not mean less of a cake.
Please feel free to reduce the sugar content even more if
you want to – I do so at home sometimes, and the results
are fine. I also substitute plain (all-purpose) flour with
wholemeal (wholewheat) flour, or add sesame and wheatgerm
to make them more nourishing. Making a great cake is not
just about sweetness, it's about flavour and texture.

We bake most of our cakes in long rectangular tins, which
makes them easier to sell in slices. They also look quite
lovely, all lined up on the counter. But you can bake them
in whatever shape of tin you prefer – rectangular, square or
round. You can make one large cake, or two medium-sized
ones, or even eight small individual cakes.

FRESH FROM THE OVEN

CARROT CAKE

This has to be a number one best-seller and probably got **Rose Bakery** noticed and talked about when we first opened.

Serves 8
unsalted butter, for greasing
4 eggs
225 g (generous 1 cup) **caster** (superfine) **sugar**
300 ml (1¼ cups) **sunflower oil**
4–5 medium carrots, finely grated
300 g (2 cups) **plain** (all-purpose) **flour, sifted**
1 teaspoon ground cinnamon
1 rounded teaspoon baking powder
½ teaspoon bicarbonate of soda (baking soda)
½ teaspoon salt
150 g (1½ cups) **finely chopped walnuts**

For the icing
125 g (generous ½ cup) **unsalted butter, softened**
250 g (generous 1 cup) **cream cheese**
½ teaspoon natural vanilla extract
50–75 g (½–¾ cup) **icing** (confectioner's) **sugar,**
   depending on how sweet you like your icing

Preheat the oven to **180°C / 350°F / Gas Mark 4.**

Butter a 23 cm (9 inch) **cake tin and line its base with parchment paper.**

Beat the eggs and caster sugar until they are light and fluffy but not too white and meringue-like.

Pour in the oil and beat for a few more minutes.

Fold in the carrots and then the flour with the cinnamon, baking powder, bicarbonate of soda and salt. Finally fold in the walnuts.

Pour the mixture into the prepared tin and bake for about 45 minutes or until a knife inserted in the centre comes out clean.

Remove from the oven and cool the cake in the tin before taking it out.

To make the icing, beat the butter with the cream cheese for a few minutes till the mixture is smooth.

Add the vanilla extract and icing sugar.

When the cake is cold, ice the top with the icing – it can be as smooth or rough as you like.

CARROT CAKE

LEMON CAKE

We make this lemony cake in a loaf tin, but it can be made in a tin of any shape. It is based on a traditional 'quatre quarts' or four quarters recipe, but I have changed some of the quantities.

Serves 8
250 g (generous 1 cup) **unsalted butter, softened, plus extra for greasing**
200 g (1 cup) **caster** (superfine) **sugar**
4 eggs
1 teaspoon natural vanilla extract
juice of 1 lemon
grated zest of 2 lemons
1 rounded teaspoon baking powder
½ teaspoon salt
50 g (scant ½ cup) **ground almonds**
280 g (scant 2 cups) **plain** (all-purpose) **flour, sifted**

For the glaze (optional)
juice of 1 lemon
about 150 g (1¼ cup) **icing** (confectioner's) **sugar**

Preheat the oven to 180°C/350°F/Gas Mark 4.

Butter a 25 cm (10 inch) loaf tin and line its base with parchment paper.

Beat the butter and caster sugar until the mixture is very light and creamy.

Add the eggs, one at a time, beating well after each addition, and the vanilla extract.

Add the lemon juice and zest.

Mix together the baking powder, salt and ground almonds and carefully fold into the mixture with the flour.

Pour the mixture into the prepared tin and bake for about 35 minutes or until a knife inserted in the centre comes out clean and the top is light golden.

Remove from the oven and cool the cake in the tin before taking it out.

Make the glaze, if you wish. Combine the lemon juice with enough icing sugar to make a thick but pourable mixture. Pour it over the cake and let it drip down the sides.

Variations
You can add the following to the cake mixture:
* A number of handfuls of blueberries, raspberries or blackberries. Fold them gently into the cake mixture and keep some back for the top.
* 2 thinly sliced apples pan-fried in unsalted butter and cinnamon. Layer them with the cake mixture to make a spiced apple cake.
* The grated zest of 2 oranges instead of the lemon zest and juice.

BANANA CAKE

You need very ripe bananas for this cake.

Serves 8
150 g (scant ¾ cup) **unsalted butter, softened, plus extra for greasing**
180 g (scant 1 cup) **caster** (superfine) **sugar**
3 eggs
3 bananas, about 350 g (12 ounces) **total weight, mashed**
110 ml (scant ½ cup) **buttermilk, or a mixture of milk and natural** (plain) **yogurt**
1 heaped teaspoon bicarbonate of soda (baking soda)
½ teaspoon salt
350 g (2⅓ cups) **plain** (all-purpose) **flour, sifted**
100 g (1 cup) **chopped walnuts**

Preheat the oven to 180°C/350°F/Gas Mark 4.

Butter a 25 cm (10 inch) loaf tin and line its base with parchment paper.

Beat the butter and sugar until they are light and creamy.

Add the eggs, one at a time, beating well after each addition.

Mix in the bananas and the buttermilk or milk and yogurt.

Mix together the bicarbonate of soda and salt and carefully fold into the mixture with the flour, then fold in the walnuts.

Using a large spoon or spatula, combine the mixture well and spoon into the prepared tin.

Bake for about 45 minutes or until a knife inserted in the centre comes out clean.

Remove from the oven and cool the cake in the tin before taking it out.

Variation
Chocolate and Banana Cake
Use the same recipe, and add 1 tablespoon cocoa powder to the flour. Fold in 200 g (7 ounces) chopped dark (bittersweet) chocolate at the same time as the walnuts.

ZESTING LEMONS

ORANGE ALMOND CAKES

These cakes are made without flour, and are very much appreciated by those who are on a gluten-free diet. We make them as little individual cakes, but you can make one large one in a 23 cm (9 inch) tin – the baking time will be 45–50 minutes.

Serves 8
unsalted butter, for greasing
2 oranges
1 lemon
6 eggs
450 g (2¼ cups) **caster** (superfine) **sugar**
550 g (5½ cups) **ground almonds, or** 450 g (4½ cups) **ground almonds mixed with** 100 g (1 cup) **ground pistachios**
1 rounded teaspoon baking powder
confit d'orange (orange glacé) **or toasted sliced almonds, to decorate**

For the apricot glaze
250 g (generous ¾ cup) **apricot jam**

Preheat the oven to 180°C/350°F/Gas Mark 4.

Butter eight individual tins and line the bases with parchment paper.

Put the oranges and lemon in a saucepan and cover with water. Place a lid on and bring to the boil, then turn the heat down and simmer for about 1 hour, or until the fruit can be pierced easily.

Deseed the oranges and lemon, put them in a food processor and process to make a purée. Put in a bowl and set aside.

In another bowl, beat the eggs and sugar until they are just combined – don't overbeat them as this will aerate the mixture too much.

Add the orange and lemon purée and finally fold in the ground almonds, or the mixture of ground almonds and ground pistachios, with the baking powder.

Mix well, spoon into the prepared tins and bake for about 35 minutes or until a knife inserted in the centre of one of the cakes comes out clean.

Remove from the oven and cool the cakes in their tins before taking them out.

To make the apricot glaze, put the jam in a saucepan with 50 ml (¼ cup) water and bring to the boil over a high heat. Keep on this high heat for a short while until it reduces and is at a high bubble, then strain the glaze to remove any lumps.

Immediately brush the cakes with the glaze while it is hot.

Decorate with confit d'orange or toasted sliced almonds.

THE WEEKDAY AFTERNOON CROWD

FRESH GINGER CAKE

This is a cross between a cake and a bread and is not at all sweet. However, it is hot with ginger, fresh and ground. It is wonderful toasted and eaten warm with butter. The cake keeps well for a few days in a sealed tin.

Serves 8
70 g (⅓ cup) **unsalted butter**, softened, plus extra for greasing
110 g (¾ cup) **plain** (all-purpose) **flour**
100 g (scant ⅔ cup) **wholemeal** (wholewheat) **flour**
1 teaspoon baking powder
1 teaspoon ground cinnamon
½ teaspoon ground mixed spice
pinch of cayenne pepper
2 rounded tablespoons ground ginger
¼ teaspoon salt
70 g (⅓ cup) **dark brown sugar**
2 tablespoons honey or golden syrup (or light corn syrup)
2 tablespoons grated fresh ginger
2 tablespoons molasses
¾ teaspoon bicarbonate of soda (baking soda)
2 eggs, beaten

Preheat the oven to **180°C / 350°F / Gas Mark 4.**

Butter a **25 cm** (10 inch) **loaf tin** and line its base with parchment paper.

In a bowl, sift the dry ingredients together: both flours, and the baking powder, cinnamon, mixed spice, cayenne, ground ginger and salt.

In another bowl, beat together the butter, sugar, honey or golden syrup and fresh ginger.

In a third bowl beat the molasses with ½ teaspoon of the bicarbonate of soda and add this to the butter-and-sugar mixture.

In a jug, combine the remaining ¼ teaspoon of bicarbonate of soda with **175 ml** (¾ cup) boiling water.

Pour it all into the butter-and-sugar mixture, and mix well.

Add all of the dry ingredients and fold in well, then mix in the eggs.

Pour the mixture into the prepared tin and bake for about 35 minutes or until a knife inserted in the centre comes out clean.

Remove from the oven and cool the cake in the tin before taking it out.

LEMON, RICE AND POLENTA CAKE

Another gluten-free cake which has a great texture and remains moist for about five days! It is best not to make a large cake as it tends to sink in the middle. Try using smaller tins – we like to use small loaf ones about **15 cm** (6 inches) **by 6 cm** (2½ inches).

Serves 8
500 g (2¼ cups) **unsalted butter**, softened, plus extra for greasing
450 g (2¼ cups) **caster** (superfine) **sugar**
grated zest of 4 lemons
juice of 1 lemon
1 teaspoon natural vanilla extract
6 eggs
550 g (5½ cups) **ground almonds**
220 g (2 cups) **polenta**
100 g (½ cup) **rice or maize** (corn) **flour**
2 teaspoons baking powder
½ teaspoon salt
icing (confectioner's) **sugar, to decorate**

Preheat the oven to **160°C / 325°F / Gas Mark 3.**

Butter eight individual tins and line the bases with parchment paper.

Beat the butter and caster sugar till they are very light and creamy, and add the lemon zest and juice and the vanilla extract. Add the eggs, one by one, beating well after each addition.

Mix together the ground almonds, polenta, rice or maize flour, baking powder and salt and fold into the mixture.

Spoon the mixture into the prepared tins and bake for about 35–40 minutes or until a knife inserted in the centre of one the cakes comes out clean.

Remove from the oven and cool the cakes in their tins before taking them out.

Sift some icing sugar over the cakes.

FRUIT CAKE & LEMON, RICE AND POLENTA CAKE

FRUIT CAKE (CHRISTMAS CAKE)

We make this cake every year for Christmas and also serve it undecorated throughout the winter months. Sometimes we leave out the whisky/brandy or add chopped almonds. As long as the basic recipe stays the same, you can add or take away any of the fruit ingredients. We normally make the cake two to three weeks before it's needed, but you can make it anything up to three months earlier. The longer, the better, as the flavours intensify and the cake seems to get more moist. For the Christmas cake, we simply brush the top with apricot glaze (see page 132), decorate it with dried fruit and nuts and then brush on some more glaze. We are not too fond of royal icing and small plastic Christmas trees.

Serves 6–8
250 g (generous 1½ cups) **sultanas** (golden raisins)
250 g (1⅔ cups) **currants**
130 g (scant ¾ cup) **raisins**
100 g (generous ½ cup) **chopped mixed peel**
    (candied citrus peel)
1 apple, peeled and grated
3 tablespoons marmalade
50 ml (¼ cup) **whisky or brandy**
grated zest and juice of 1 lemon
grated zest and juice of 1 orange
125 g (generous ½ cup) **unsalted butter, softened,**
    plus extra for greasing
125 g (⅔ cup) **soft brown sugar**
2 tablespoons treacle (or molasses)
3 eggs
150 g (1 cup) **plain** (all-purpose) **flour, sifted**
100 g (1 cup) **ground almonds**
1 rounded teaspoon ground cinnamon
1 rounded teaspoon ground mixed spice
½ teaspoon salt

Combine the sultanas, currants, raisins, chopped peel, apple, marmalade, whisky or brandy, lemon zest and juice, and orange zest and juice and soak overnight.

Preheat the oven to 160°C/325°F/Gas Mark 3.

Butter a 25 cm (10 inch) cake tin and line its base and sides with parchment paper.

Beat the butter and sugar till they are light. Mix in the treacle, then add the eggs, one at a time, beating well after each addition.

Fold in the flour, ground almonds, cinnamon, mixed spice and salt. Finally fold in the fruit mixture.

Spoon into the prepared tin and bake for about 1½ hours.

Keep checking after 1 hour: when a knife inserted in the centre comes out clean the cake is ready.

Remove from the oven, cool the cake in the tin and then take it out and wrap in foil till required.

Make sure you keep turning the cake to ensure the whisky or brandy spreads evenly through it.

APPLES FROM CHEGWORTH VALLEY FARM

VEGAN FRUIT CAKE

I love the dense texture of this cake with its slight taste of spices.

Serves 6–8
180 g (1 cup) **chopped dried apricots**
180 g (1 cup) **chopped stoned dates**
150 g (¾ cup) **chopped dried figs**
180 ml (¾ cup) **sunflower oil,**
  plus extra for greasing
150 g (scant 1 cup) **sultanas** (golden raisins)
2 **bananas, mashed**
200 ml (scant 1 cup) **orange or apple juice**
80 g (2 tablespoons) **molasses sugar or**
  dark brown sugar
grated zest of 1 lemon
400 g (scant 2½ cups) **self-raising wholemeal**
  (wholewheat) **flour**
2 rounded teaspoons **ground mixed spice**

Soften the apricots, dates and figs in 400 ml (1¾ cups) **warm water** for about 30 minutes.

Preheat the oven to 180°C/350°F/Gas Mark 4.

Oil a 25 cm (10 inch) **loaf tin** and line its base and sides with parchment paper.

Drain the fruits, and set aside the soaking liquid in case you need it later.

Put the fruits in a bowl, and add the sultanas, bananas, orange or apple juice, oil, sugar and lemon zest. Set aside.

In another bowl, sift together the flour and mixed spice.

Mix these dry ingredients into the wet fruit mixture and stir carefully to get a soft, wet consistency. If the mixture is too dry and stiff add some of the soaking liquid.

Spoon into the prepared tin and bake the cake for about 45–60 minutes or until a knife inserted in the centre comes out clean.

Remove from the oven and cool the cake in the tin before taking it out.

PISTACHIO CAKE

I call this 'Tilly's Cake' as we worked on it together when she was working with us for a while, on a break from Trinity College, Dublin. Our first attempts, without flour, shrunk a lot and were difficult to control, so we finally gave up and added the flour. But the cake remains moist and delicious all the same.
Thank you, Tilly.

Serves 6–8
250 g (generous 1 cup) **unsalted butter, softened,**
  plus extra for greasing
225 g (generous 1 cup) **caster** (superfine) **sugar**
grated zest of 1 lemon
2 tablespoons **natural rosewater** or ½ teaspoon
  natural vanilla extract
4 **eggs**
100 g (1 cup) **ground almonds**
100 g (1 cup) **ground pistachios**
50 g (⅓ cup) **plain** (all-purpose) **flour**
1 teaspoon **baking powder**
pinch of salt

For the topping
50 g (½ cup) **pistachios, whole or chopped**
50 g (¼ cup) **caster** (superfine) **sugar**
grated zest and juice of 1 lemon

Preheat the oven to 180°C/350°F/Gas Mark 4.

Butter a 25 cm (10 inch) **cake tin** and line its base and sides with parchment paper.

Beat the butter and sugar until they are very light and creamy. Mix in the lemon zest and rosewater or vanilla extract. Add the eggs, one at a time, beating well after each addition.

Now fold in the ground almonds, ground pistachios, flour, baking powder and salt.

Pour the mixture into the prepared tin and bake for about 40 minutes or until a knife inserted in the centre comes out clean.

Remove from the oven and cool the cake in the tin before taking it out.

To make the topping, gently heat the pistachios, sugar and lemon zest and juice in a saucepan and pour over the cake.

PISTACHIO CAKE

RICOTTA CHEESECAKE

This is inspired by Italian cheesecakes, not the American versions. It is smooth and creamy but not as rich as the American cakes, and it takes on the slightly grainy texture of the ricotta. It is best eaten on the day it is prepared, but will keep well for a few days in the fridge.

Serves 8
unsalted butter, for greasing
800 g (3½ cups) **ricotta cheese**
200 g (scant 1 cup) **cream cheese**
130 g (⅔ cup) **caster** (superfine) **sugar**
grated zest and juice of 2 lemons
1 teaspoon natural vanilla extract
pinch of ground cinnamon
5 eggs
1 egg yolk
200 ml (scant 1 cup) **single** (light) **cream**
1 tablespoon **plain** (all-purpose) **flour**

For the base
180 g (7 ounces) **digestive biscuits** (graham crackers)**, crushed**
60 g (¼ cup) **unsalted butter, melted**
pinch of ground cinnamon or ground ginger

Preheat the oven to 180°C / 350°F / Gas Mark 4.

Butter a 25 cm (10 inch) cake tin with a removable base and line its base and sides with parchment paper.

To make the base for the cheesecake, mix the digestive biscuits with the butter and ground cinnamon or ginger and press the mixture over the base of the tin.

Mix all the ingredients for the filling together in the following order: the cheeses, sugar, lemon zest and juice, vanilla extract, cinnamon, eggs and egg yolk, cream and flour. Make sure there are no lumps in the mixture.

Pour into the prepared tin, over the biscuit base, and bake for about 45 minutes, or until just set. The filling must not get golden on top – it should be pale and just beginning to puff up.

Remove from the oven and cool the cheesecake in the tin before taking it out.

RICOTTA CHEESECAKE

ARTICHOKE AND TOMATO CAKE

This cake needs to be eaten on the day it is prepared as it does not keep very well.

Serves 8
unsalted butter, for greasing
4–5 globe artichokes
salt and ground black pepper
10 tomatoes, halved
300 g (2 cups) plain (all-purpose) flour, sifted
2 teaspoons baking powder
6 eggs
200 ml (scant 1 cup) milk
200 ml (scant 1 cup) sunflower oil
200 g (2 cups) grated Parmesan cheese
1 handful pine nuts (optional)

Preheat the oven to 180°C/350°F/Gas Mark 4.

Butter a 25 cm (10 inch) loaf tin and line its base and sides with parchment paper.

Prepare the artichokes. Remove the stalks and the tips of the outer leaves, and cook the artichokes in salted boiling water for about 30 minutes.

Remove the tough outer leaves and the chokes and cut the artichokes into slices. Set aside.

Meanwhile roast the tomatoes in the oven for about 30 minutes, till all the liquid has gone – then peel them and season with salt and pepper. Set aside. Keep the oven switched on.

Mix together the flour and the baking powder.

Beat the eggs in a bowl, then mix in the flour and baking powder. Don't overmix – everything must just come together smoothly.

Add the milk and oil, and finally fold in the Parmesan and the artichokes and tomatoes.

Spoon carefully into the prepared tin and sprinkle with the pine nuts, if you wish.

Bake for about 40 minutes or until a knife inserted in the centre comes out clean.

Remove from the oven and cool the cake in the tin before taking it out.

BROCCOLI CAKE

It is only recently that I have started doing 'savoury' cakes, mainly because I didn't know when people would eat them. They are certainly not ideal at tea-time! But we have been selling them well for evening receptions. This recipe was inspired by Guy Martin's broccoli cake, from his wonderful book 'Legumes'.

Serves 8
500 g (2¼ cups) unsalted butter, softened, plus extra for greasing
800 g (1 pound 12 ounces) broccoli, cut into florets
100 g (½ cup) caster (superfine) sugar
7 eggs
550 g (3⅔ cups) plain (all-purpose) flour, sifted
1½ teaspoons baking powder
1 rounded teaspoon ground turmeric
pinch of cayenne pepper
1 teaspoon curry powder
½ teaspoon salt

Preheat the oven to 180°C/350°F/Gas Mark 4.

Butter a 25 cm (10 inch) loaf tin and line its base and sides with parchment paper.

Blanch the broccoli in boiling water for about 3 minutes, then drain well and set aside.

Beat the butter till it is very light and creamy, then beat in the sugar.

Add the eggs, one at a time, beating well after each addition.

Mix together the baking powder, turmeric, cayenne, curry powder and salt, and fold into the mixture with the flour. Mix well and spoon into the prepared tin.

Push the broccoli into the mixture – be quite generous so that each slice will have a good number of florets.

Bake for about 45 minutes or until a knife inserted in the centre comes out clean.

Remove from the oven and cool the cake in the tin before taking it out – but eat on the same day. This cake does not keep very well.

BROCCOLI CAKE

BISCUITS AND COOKIES

We have found that the quickest way to sell biscuits and cookies is to place them on the counter when they are still hot and on their baking trays…the smell of warm vanilla, cinnamon, chocolate or ginger makes them utterly irresistible.

It is quite rare to find freshly baked biscuits like ours in retail, and ever since we found the right packaging for them – a way of tying cellophane bags so that they stay fresh – we haven't looked back. They keep for two weeks in airtight containers, or can be stored in the fridge for a few days until needed. However, there really is nothing like biscuits and cookies fresh out of the oven, and they are really so simple to make.

JACOB, OUR KITCHEN ASSISTANT

PECAN BISCUITS

These are wonderfully light and can be made with walnuts instead of pecans.

Makes about 24 biscuits
220 g (scant 1 cup) **unsalted butter,
  plus extra for greasing**
150 g (generous 1 cup) **pecan nuts**
50 g (¼ cup) **caster** (superfine) **sugar, plus
  1 tablespoon**
1 teaspoon natural vanilla extract
300 g (2 cups) **plain** (all-purpose) **flour, sifted**
icing (confectioner's) **sugar, to decorate**

Preheat the oven to **180°C / 350°F / Gas Mark 4.**

Butter a baking tray and line it with parchment paper.

Place the nuts on another baking tray and roast them for about 15 minutes. When they begin to give off a nutty smell take them out and grind them finely with 1 tablespoon caster sugar. Put aside to cool. Keep the oven switched on.

Beat the butter with 50 g caster sugar till light and fluffy, then add the vanilla extract.

Fold in the flour and lastly the ground nuts.

If the dough is too soft put it in the fridge to chill for about 15 minutes.

Break off pieces of dough and shape them into 2 cm (¾ inch) balls.

Place on the prepared tray and bake for about 15 minutes or until lightly golden.

As soon as you take the biscuits out of the oven sprinkle them with icing sugar.

Cool.

SHORTBREAD

Dead simple. Delicious!

Makes about 24 biscuits
250 g (generous 1 cup) **cold unsalted butter,
  plus extra for greasing**
100 g (½ cup) **caster** (superfine) **sugar**
**1 teaspoon natural vanilla extract or grated
  zest of 1 lemon**
225 g (1⅓ cups) **plain** (all-purpose) **flour,
  plus extra for dusting**
60 g (½ cup) **rice flour**
pinch of salt

Butter a baking tray and line it with parchment paper.

Bring together the butter, sugar, vanilla extract or lemon zest, the plain and rice flours and the salt. Mix until the dough just comes together.

Turn out the dough on a lightly floured surface and knead a little until it is smooth and well blended.

Roll out to about 5 mm (¼ inch) thick and cut into shapes. At Rose Bakery we use a flower-shaped cutter.

Place on the prepared tray and chill for about 1 hour.

Preheat the oven to **160°C / 325°F / Gas Mark 3,** then bake the biscuits for 15–20 minutes until just turning golden. The shortbread must be cooked but should remain pale.

Cool.

SHORTBREAD

ALMOND, CINNAMON AND MERINGUE BISCUITS

These are inspired by the Austrian star biscuits you find at Christmas, but our customers ask for them all year round. They are a little tricky to cut, and you have to be very careful with the timing as they must be cooked but still chewy. My staff are always around when we make these and end up eating any scraps that are lying about, cooked or raw! An added bonus: they are gluten-free.

Makes 40–50 biscuits
4 egg whites
450 g (4½ cups) **icing** (confectioner's) **sugar,**
  plus extra for dusting
juice of ½ lemon and grated zest of 1 lemon
320 g (3⅓ cups) **ground almonds**
100 g (generous ½ cup) **finely chopped mixed peel**
  (candied citrus peel)
1 teaspoon ground cinnamon
unsalted butter, for greasing

First make the meringue. Beat the egg whites until they form stiff peaks, then, very gradually, add the sugar. When the mixture is very stiff, beat in the lemon juice.

Set aside 200 g (6 ounces) of the meringue for the topping and put the remaining meringue in a bowl.

Add the ground almonds, mixed peel, cinnamon and lemon zest.

Mix until you have a dough-like paste, then chill in the fridge for 1 hour.

Butter a baking tray and line it with parchment paper.

Dust your work surface with sugar and roll the paste out to make a sheet 1 cm (½ inch) thick. Cut into your desired shapes (stars, squares or rounds).

Brush the tops with the reserved meringue and leave to dry on the prepared baking tray for about 1 hour.

Preheat the oven to 180°C/350°F/Gas Mark 4 and bake the biscuits for about 10 minutes, until the bases are lightly golden. The tops should remain white and the bases must be soft and moist.

Cool and enjoy.

ALMOND, CINNAMON AND MERINGUE BISCUITS

HOT GINGERNUT BISCUITS

I have always loved these biscuits. I used to buy them from **Sally Clarke's** shop, '**& Clarkes**', on **Kensington Church Street** in London, and when we opened **Rose Bakery** I asked her if she would mind giving me the recipe. She very kindly agreed. This is her recipe, with a little less sugar and a little more ginger! If you think the biscuits may be too hot for you, don't add the cayenne.

Makes about 24 biscuits
200 g (scant 1 cup) **unsalted butter, softened,** plus extra for greasing
440 g (scant 3 cups) **self-raising** (self-rising) **flour**
150 g (¾ cup) **caster** (superfine) **sugar**
3 tablespoons ground ginger
pinch of cayenne pepper (optional)
1½ tablespoons bicarbonate of soda (baking soda)
240 g (8 ounces) **golden syrup** (or light corn syrup), warmed
40 g (2 ounces) **treacle** (or molasses), **warmed**

Preheat the oven to 160°C / 325°F / Gas Mark 3.

Butter a baking tray or line it with parchment paper.

If you are using a food processor, process the flour with the sugar, ground ginger, cayenne if using, bicarbonate of soda and butter until they are well mixed. Otherwise, cut the butter into small pieces, mix the dry ingredients together and rub the butter into them with your fingers, and bring together to make a dough.

Add the golden syrup and treacle.

Break off pieces and shape them into 3 cm (1¼ inch) **balls**.

Place well apart on the prepared tray and bake for about 10 minutes. The biscuits will rise and then fall a little. They must be crisp on the outside and a little chewy on the inside.

Cool.

CHOCOLATE CHIP BISCUITS

These are classic biscuits that sell without even trying. The chocolate we use for them is 70 per cent cocoa solids.

Makes about 25 biscuits
225 g (1 cup) **unsalted butter, softened,** plus extra for greasing
220 g (generous 1 cup) **caster** (superfine) **sugar**
1 teaspoon natural vanilla extract
2 eggs
½ teaspoon salt
½ teaspoon bicarbonate of soda (baking soda)
360 g (generous 2⅓ cups) **plain** (all-purpose) **flour,** sifted, plus extra for dusting
250 g (9 ounces) **chopped chocolate**

Beat the butter with the sugar till light and fluffy, then add the vanilla extract.

Add the eggs, one at a time, beating well after each addition.

Mix together the salt and bicarbonate of soda, and fold into the mixture with the flour.

Finally fold in the chocolate and mix till smooth.

On a lightly floured surface, roll the dough out into a log shape 4 cm (1½ inches) **wide,** and chill in the fridge for about 2 hours till hard.

Preheat the oven to 180°C / 350°F / Gas Mark 4.

Butter a baking tray and line it with parchment paper.

Cut the dough into 5 mm (¼ inch) slices and place them well apart on the prepared tray.

Bake for about 10 minutes or until lightly golden.

Cool.

CHOCOLATE CHIP BISCUITS

PEANUT BUTTER AND CHOCOLATE CHIP BISCUITS

Makes about 25 biscuits
200 g (scant 1 cup) **unsalted butter, softened,**
  plus extra for greasing
200 g (1 cup) **crunchy peanut butter**
250 g (1¼ cups) **soft light brown sugar**
1 teaspoon **natural vanilla extract**
2 **eggs**
335 g (2¼ cups) **plain** (all-purpose) **flour, sifted,**
  plus extra for dusting
1 teaspoon **salt**
1 teaspoon **bicarbonate of soda** (baking soda)
250 g (9 ounces) **chopped chocolate**

Beat the butter with the peanut butter and sugar till light, then add the vanilla extract.

Add the eggs, one at a time, beating well after each addition.

Fold in the flour and salt.

Mix the bicarbonate of soda with 1 teaspoon hot water and quickly add this to the mixture.

Finally, fold in the chocolate.

On a lightly floured surface, roll the dough out into a log shape 4 cm (1½ inches) **wide,** and chill in the fridge for about 2 hours till hard.

Preheat the oven to 180°C/350°F/Gas Mark 4.

Butter a baking tray and line it with parchment paper.

Cut the dough into 5 mm (¼ inch) **slices** and place them well apart on the prepared tray.

Bake until pale golden.

Cool.

ROLLED FRUIT COOKIES

We discovered these Jewish cookies, also known as Rugelach, in New York and they are so delicious it's surprising we don't find them more often in Europe. I like them because the pastry is made with cream cheese and very little sugar, so even though the filling is quite sweet, the cookie is not.

Makes about 12–15 cookies
150 g (⅔ cup) **unsalted butter, softened,**
  plus extra for greasing
150 g (⅔ cup) **cream cheese or curd cheese**
1 tablespoon **caster** (superfine) **sugar**
pinch of **salt**
220 g (1½ cups) **plain** (all-purpose) **flour, sifted,**
  plus extra for dusting
about 3 tablespoons **apricot jam**
1 **egg, beaten, for glazing**
ground cinnamon mixed with **caster** (superfine)
  sugar, to decorate (optional)

For the filling
100 g (1 cup) **chopped walnuts**
50 g (¼ cup) **caster** (superfine) **sugar**
2 teaspoons **ground cinnamon**
160 g (1 cup) **chopped sultanas** (golden raisins)
  or raisins

Make the dough first as it has to chill. Beat the butter with the cream cheese or curd cheese till smooth and light. Add the sugar and salt, then fold in the flour and form into a manageable dough.

Wrap in cling film (plastic wrap) **and chill in** the fridge for about 2 hours.

Meanwhile, prepare the filling. Preheat the oven to 180°C/350°F/Gas Mark 4, place the walnuts on a baking tray and roast them for about 15 minutes.

Cool, then mix with the sugar, cinnamon and sultanas or raisins.

On a lightly floured surface, roll the dough out into a rectangle about 40 cm (16 inches) **long and 15 cm** (6 inches) **wide, and about** 5 mm (¼ inch) **thick.**

Spread the dough with a thin layer of apricot jam.

Sprinkle with the filling, press it into the jam, and roll up the dough from the short end to form a log, making at least three turns.

Wrap in cling film and chill the log in the fridge for about 1 hour.

Preheat the oven to 180°C/350°F/Gas Mark 4.

Butter a baking tray and line it with parchment paper.

Cut the log into 2 cm (¾ inch) **slices and** lightly brush the sides with the beaten egg. Sprinkle a little mixed cinnamon and sugar over the slices if you wish.

Place on the prepared tray and bake for 20–30 minutes until golden. Make sure the undersides of the cookies don't burn.

Cool.

ROLLED FRUIT COOKIES

PINE NUT AND ALMOND BISCUITS

Another gluten-free recipe, this time from the south of France. The biscuits keep well for a few weeks in an airtight container.

Makes about 20 biscuits
unsalted butter, for greasing
350 g (3½ cups) ground almonds
350 g (1¾ cups) caster (superfine) sugar
3 eggs, separated (1 or 2 extra egg yolks may be needed)
300 g (3 cups) pine nuts

Preheat the oven to 160°C / 325°F / Gas Mark 3.

Butter a baking tray and line it with parchment paper.

Mix together the ground almonds and the sugar.

Lightly beat the egg whites until they are well mixed and starting to be frothy and add them to the almond-and-sugar mixture to make a paste.

Break off pieces and shape them into 2.5 cm (1 inch) balls.

Lightly beat the 3 egg yolks (you may need more yolks).

Put the pine nuts in a bowl.

Roll the balls in the beaten egg yolks, then roll them in the pine nuts.

Place on the prepared tray and bake for about 25 minutes until light golden.

Cool.

GINGERBREAD BISCUITS

These are very popular ginger biscuits as they are not too sweet. At Christmas, we decorate them with lines of white icing.

Makes 15–25 biscuits, depending on cutter size
125 g (generous ½ cup) unsalted butter, softened, plus extra for greasing
90 g (½ cup) brown sugar
3 tablespoons molasses
1 egg, beaten
370 g (2½ cups) plain (all-purpose) flour, sifted
1 teaspoon bicarbonate of soda (baking soda)
½ teaspoon salt
1 tablespoon ground ginger
1 teaspoon ground cinnamon
1 teaspoon ground mixed spice

Beat the butter with the sugar and molasses till light and well mixed.

Add the egg, then fold in the flour and other dry ingredients, sifted together. The mixture should come together easily. If it is too wet, add a little more flour; if it is too dry, add one more egg.

Put the dough in the fridge for 30 minutes to chill.

Preheat the oven to 180°C / 350°F / Gas Mark 4.

Butter a baking tray and line it with parchment paper.

Roll out the dough to about 5 mm (¼ inch) thick.

Cut into your desired shapes and place on the prepared tray.

Bake for about 10–15 minutes until slightly firm.

Cool.

GINGERBREAD BISCUITS

OAT AND COCONUT COOKIES

These are based on the Australian cookies known as 'Anzacs'.

Makes about 24 biscuits
125g (generous ½ cup) unsalted butter, plus extra for greasing
160g (1 cup) wholemeal (wholewheat) flour
100g (generous 1 cup) desiccated (dried) coconut
180g (scant 1 cup) light brown sugar
100g (1⅓ cups) rolled oats
pinch of salt
1 tablespoon golden syrup (or light corn syrup)
½ teaspoon bicarbonate of soda (baking soda)

Preheat the oven to 160°C / 325°F / Gas Mark 3. Butter a baking tray or line it with parchment paper.

Put the dry ingredients in a bowl and mix well.

Put the butter and golden syrup in a saucepan and cook over a low heat, stirring, until the butter has melted.

Mix the bicarbonate of soda with 2 tablespoons boiling water and add to the butter and golden syrup. Pour this over the dry ingredients and bring them together to form a dough.

Break off pieces and shape them into 3cm (1¼ inch) balls.

Place well apart on the prepared tray and bake for about 15 minutes until golden. Do not overbake as the cookies must be slightly chewy.

Cool.

JAM SANDWICH VEGAN COOKIES

Use a good jam or preserve for this, as the flavour is all in the filling. The vegan margarine should be soya (soy) based, and not made from hydrogenated oils.

Makes about 12–15 cookies
100g (1 cup) whole almonds
oil, for greasing
150g (scant 1 cup) self-raising wholemeal (wholewheat) flour
150g (2 cups) rolled oats
150g (¾ cup) light brown sugar
160g (scant ¾ cup) vegan margarine
about 4 tablespoons jam

Preheat the oven to 180°C / 350°F / Gas Mark 4.

Place the almonds on a baking tray and roast them for about 15 minutes, stirring them once or twice. Remove and keep the oven switched on.

Cool and chop the almonds. Set aside.

Oil a 20 x 28cm (8 x 11 inch) baking tray and line it with parchment paper.

If you are using a food processor, process the flour, oats, sugar and margarine until the mixture is crumbly. Otherwise, cut the margarine into small pieces, mix the dry ingredients together and rub the margarine into them with your fingers.

Place half the mixture on the prepared tray and spread the jam over it.

Add the chopped almonds to the remaining mixture and sprinkle over the jam.

Bake for about 25–30 minutes until golden.

Cool on the tray, then cut into squares.

RECSI SCALES

ECCLES CAKES

These traditional English cakes were originally
made with lard, but I have substituted butter.

Makes 18 cakes
500 g (3⅓ cups) **plain** (all-purpose) **flour**
pinch of salt
280 g (1¼ cups) **cold unsalted butter,**
 plus extra for greasing
about 250 ml (1 cup) **water**

For the Eccles mixture
200 g (1½ cups) **currants**
90 g (generous ⅓ cup) **unsalted butter**
90 g (½ cup) **brown sugar**
1 rounded teaspoon ground ginger
2 rounded teaspoons ground mixed spice
grated zest of 1 lemon
shot of whisky (optional)

For glazing
1 egg, beaten
1 tablespoon caster (superfine) **sugar**

First make the pastry. Sift together the flour
and salt, then cut the butter into the flour
until the pieces are about the size of almonds.
Pour in just enough water to bring the dough
together, adding more if you need it.

Roll out the dough to a long rectangle, about
40 cm (16 inches) **long and 14 cm** (5 inches) **wide,
and 1 cm** (½ inch) **thick. Fold the dough over
into thirds. Chill for about 1 hour.**

Meanwhile, make the Eccles mixture. Put all
the ingredients in a saucepan and heat gently,
stirring often until the butter has melted.
Put aside to chill.

When you are ready to make the cakes,
preheat the oven to 200°C/400°F/Gas Mark 6.

Butter a baking tray and line it with parchment
paper. Divide the pastry into three pieces.
Roll out each one to a thickness of about
5 mm (¼ inch) **and cut out circles using a large
round cookie cutter, about 10 cm** (4 inches)
in diameter.

Put a tablespoon of the Eccles mixture in
the middle of each circle and fold the dough
up to cover. Turn them over and roll a little to
flatten into shape, taking care that the mixture
doesn't leak out underneath. Cut three little
slits into the surface.

Place on the prepared baking tray, brush with
the beaten egg and sprinkle with a little caster
sugar, then bake the cakes for about 10–15
minutes, until lightly golden and crisp.

ECCLES CAKES

At first our customers were very reluctant to buy our date and oat slices as the French are not too fond of oats. As with our carrot cake, the idea seemed strange to them. But like the carrot cake, the date and oat slices have become one of our best sellers. We make all our tray bakes in large, rectangular tins and they look wonderful lined up on the counter, begging to be eaten. You can bake the tray bakes in whatever size or shape of tin you have, but remember that they must always have a depth of 2–3 cm (1–2 inches)…otherwise they will turn into cookies or cakes!

DATE AND OAT SLICES

We use Medjool dates for these, but you can of course use other ones. Just make sure they are not too dry.

Makes about 15–20 squares
150 g (⅔ cup) **unsalted butter, plus extra for greasing**
500 g (scant 3 cups) **chopped stoned dates**
1 teaspoon **natural vanilla extract**
150 g (scant 1 cup) **wholemeal** (wholewheat) **flour**
pinch of salt
200 g (2⅓ cup) **rolled oats**
½ teaspoon **bicarbonate of soda** (baking soda)
2 tablespoons **wheatgerm (optional)**
120 g (scant ⅔ cup) **light brown sugar**
1 teaspoon **molasses**
2 tablespoons **golden syrup** (or light corn syrup)

Preheat the oven to 180°C / 350°F / Gas Mark 4.

Butter a 20 x 28 cm (8 x 11 inch) **baking tin and line it with parchment paper.**

Put the dates in a saucepan with 200 ml (scant 1 cup) **water and cook over a low heat, stirring occasionally, until the dates are soft and have absorbed all the water.**

Stir in the vanilla extract and set aside.

In a bowl, mix the flour with the salt, oats and bicarbonate of soda. I sometimes add wheatgerm at this stage.

Put the butter, sugar, molasses and golden syrup in another saucepan and cook over a low heat, stirring, until melted. Pour this into the oat mixture and mix till crumbly.

Press half the mixture into the base of the prepared tin.

Spread the dates evenly over the top and sprinkle with the remaining oat mixture.

Bake for about 30 minutes or until golden.

Cool in the tin, and cut into slices when cold.

COCONUT CUSTARD SLICES

Makes 15–20 squares
125 g (generous ½ cup) **unsalted butter, softened, plus extra for greasing**
100 g (½ cup) **caster** (superfine) **sugar**
1 egg
1 teaspoon **natural vanilla extract**
grated zest of 1 lemon
230 g (1½ cups) **plain** (all-purpose) **flour, sifted**
pinch of salt
½ teaspoon **baking powder**

For the filling
4 eggs
180 g (scant 1 cup) **caster** (superfine) **sugar**
90 g (1 cup) **desiccated** (dried) **coconut, plus extra for sprinkling (optional)**
50 g (⅓ cup) **plain** (all-purpose) **flour**
350 ml (1½ cups) **single** (light) **cream**
150 ml (⅔ cup) **coconut milk**
grated zest and juice of 2 limes

Preheat the oven to 180°C / 350°F / Gas Mark 4.

Butter a 20 x 28 cm (8 x 11 inch) **baking tin and line it with parchment paper.**

First make the base. Beat the butter with the sugar till light and creamy.

Add the egg, vanilla extract and lemon zest, then fold in the flour, with the salt and baking powder.

Press the mixture into the base of the prepared tin and bake for about 20 minutes till light golden. Set aside to cool.

Reduce the oven temperature to 160°C / 325°F / Gas Mark 3.

To make the filling, whisk the eggs with the sugar until the mixture is pale.

Add the coconut, flour, cream, coconut milk and the lime zest and juice. Mix well together and pour on to the base.

Bake for about 35 minutes or until the filling has just set.

Cool in the tin, and cut into slices only when completely cold. We sometimes sprinkle extra coconut over the slices.

DATE AND OAT SLICES

HAZELNUT BROWNIES

The chocolate we use for these is the Valrhona Guanaja 70 per cent cocoa-solid bar, which makes very luxurious brownies. When the Valrhona representative called round and discovered we used his chocolate for them – most people use cocoa powder – he was dumbstruck and delighted! So, yes, these are very rich brownies, moist and delicious. If you can't find Valrhona chocolate use the best available.

Makes 15–20 squares
120 g (generous ¾ cup) **hazelnuts**
250 g (generous 1 cup) **unsalted butter, plus extra for greasing**
250 g (9 ounces) **roughly chopped chocolate**
6 eggs
380 g (scant 2 cups) **caster** (superfine) **sugar**
1 teaspoon natural vanilla extract
150 g (1 cup) **plain** (all-purpose) **flour, sifted**
pinch of salt

Preheat the oven to 180°C/350°F/Gas Mark 4.

Place the hazelnuts on a baking tray and roast them for about 15 minutes, stirring them once or twice, until they give off a nutty smell. Remove and set aside to cool. Keep the oven switched on.

Butter a 20 x 28 cm (8 x 11 inch) baking tin and line it with parchment paper.

When the hazelnuts are cool, rub off as much of the skins as you can. Chop the nuts roughly and spread them over the base of the prepared tin.

Put the chocolate and butter in a heatproof bowl, place the bowl over a saucepan of simmering water and cook over a low heat until melted and smooth. Remove from the heat and cool slightly.

In another bowl, beat the eggs with the sugar and add the vanilla extract. Beat for only a few minutes till the mixture is well combined and just beginning to froth – it must not get to the light white stage.

Pour in the melted chocolate and butter, and finally fold in the flour and salt.

Pour the mixture evenly over the hazelnuts and bake for about 25 minutes. Be very careful not to overbake – brownies must be a little moist in the middle. The cake will continue to cook after it is taken out of the oven, so don't worry if it seems undercooked.

Cool in the tin, and cut into slices when cold.

BROWNIE CHEESECAKE

This is a variation of our Hazelnut Brownies (see left), but without the hazelnuts.

Makes 15–20 squares
250 g (generous 1 cup) **unsalted butter, plus extra for greasing**
250 g (9 ounces) **roughly chopped chocolate**
6 eggs
380 g (scant 2 cups) **caster** (superfine) **sugar**
1 teaspoon natural vanilla extract
150 g (1 cup) **plain** (all-purpose) **flour, sifted**
pinch of salt

For the cheesecake mix
125 g (generous ½ cup) **ricotta cheese**
50 g (scant ¼ cup) **cream cheese**
2 tablespoons caster (superfine) **sugar**
splash of natural vanilla extract
1 egg
5 teaspoons double (heavy) **cream**
1 tablespoon flour

Preheat the oven to 180°C/350°F/Gas Mark 4.

Butter a 20 x 28 cm (8 x 11 inch) baking tin and line it with parchment paper.

First mix all the ingredients for the cheesecake together in the following order: the cheeses, sugar, vanilla extract, egg, cream and flour. Make sure there are no lumps in the mixture, and set aside.

Put the chocolate and butter in a heatproof bowl, place the bowl over a saucepan of simmering water and cook over a low heat until melted and smooth. Remove from the heat and cool slightly.

In another bowl, beat the eggs with the sugar and add the vanilla extract. Beat for only a few minutes till the mixture is well combined and just beginning to froth – it must not get to the light white stage.

Pour in the melted chocolate and butter, and finally fold in the flour and salt.

Pour the mixture evenly into the baking tin, and swirl in the cheesecake mix. Make any design you want but don't mix in too much.

Bake for about 25 minutes. Be very careful not to overbake – brownies must be a little moist in the middle. The cake will continue to cook after it is taken out of the oven, so don't worry if it seems undercooked.

Cool in the tin, and cut into slices when cold.

BROWNIE CHEESECAKE
& HAZELNUT BROWNIES

APRICOT, ALMOND AND RICOTTA SLICES

We use apricots for this recipe but you can replace them with any fruit you like. Blueberries or peaches would be just as good, so too would juicy green figs.

Makes 15–20 squares
250 g (generous 1 cup) unsalted butter, softened, plus extra for greasing
240 g (scant 1¼ cups) caster (superfine) sugar, plus extra for sprinkling
6 eggs, separated
grated zest and juice of 3 lemons
250 g (2½ cups) ground almonds
100 g (⅔ cup) plain (all-purpose) flour
pinch of salt
350 g (1½ cups) ricotta cheese
about 12–14 apricots, halved and stoned
Apricot glaze (see page 134, optional)

Preheat the oven to 180°C/350°F/Gas Mark 4.

Butter a 20 x 28 cm (8 x 11 inch) baking tin and line it with parchment paper.

Beat the butter with the sugar till light and creamy.

Add the egg yolks, one at a time, beating well after each addition, and then the lemon zest and juice.

Sift and mix the ground almonds, flour and the salt and fold into the mixture.

In a separate bowl, beat the egg whites until they form stiff peaks, then fold them into the mixture, half the quantity at a time. Make sure you use a metal spoon so that you don't deflate the batter too much.

Finally, carefully fold in the ricotta and pour into the prepared tin.

Place the apricots, skin-side down, on top and sprinkle with a little more sugar.

Bake for about 45 minutes or until just set.

Cool in the tin, then carefully cut into slices when cold. We sometimes brush the apricots with an apricot glaze, or sprinkle a little more sugar over them while cooling.

RED BEAN SLICES

It has taken me a long time to realize this recipe – to transform what is intrinsically an Eastern taste into a Western one. Starting from what is a basic rice-and-bean concept, this delicious result can now be appreciated by most people. Once again, I have reduced the sugar content as much as I dare. To make this into a vegan recipe you can replace the butter with a vegan margarine, and use golden syrup (or light corn syrup) instead of honey. You can also use tinned, ready-cooked adzuki beans, which can be found in many wholefood stores. This saves a lot of preparation time.

Makes 15–20 squares
200 g (generous 1 cup) adzuki beans, soaked overnight in 3 times their volume of water
180 g (scant 1 cup) caster (superfine) sugar
2 tablespoons honey
1 teaspoon natural vanilla extract
150 g (⅔ cup) unsalted butter, plus extra for greasing
100 g (⅔ cup) plain (all-purpose) flour
100 g (1 cup) ground almonds
100 g (⅔ cup) rice flour
pinch of salt

Drain the beans, put them into a saucepan, cover with fresh water and bring to the boil.

Drain them again, put them back in the saucepan with the same amount of fresh water, then turn the heat down and simmer the beans for about 1½ hours till they are very soft. Keep adding water if they start to dry out and skim the surface carefully.

When the beans are completely soft, drain them and put them back in the saucepan.

Add 100 g (½ cup) of the sugar, and the honey and vanilla extract. Stir over a low heat for about 5 minutes until the sugar has dissolved.

Put into a food processor and process till smooth, or put through a sieve until the beans are paste-like in texture. Set aside to cool.

Preheat the oven to 180°C/350°F/Gas Mark 4.

Butter a 20 x 28 cm (8 x 11 inch) baking tin and line it with parchment paper.

If you are using a food processor, process the flour, ground almonds, rice flour, butter, the remaining sugar and the salt until the mixture is quite crumbly. Otherwise, cut the butter into small pieces, mix the dry ingredients together and rub the butter into them with your fingers. If the mixture is too dry, add a little more butter.

Press half the mixture into the prepared tin.

Spread the adzuki paste evenly over the top and sprinkle with the remaining flour-and-almond mixture (like a crumble). Bake for 25–30 minutes till the topping is golden and crisp.

Cool in the tin.

When cold, cut into squares. Take the slices out of the tin very carefully as the topping tends to crumble (because of the rice flour).

RED BEAN SLICES

Puddings do not have a large part to play at Rose Bakery as we have only one on the menu each day. When it comes to dessert, customers often prefer to choose from the large display of cakes and fruit salads on our counter. However, there are several puddings that we make regularly, especially in winter. They are served very simply, without flourish or swirls, and are based on traditional recipes – the kind of «comfort food» you would eat at home.

APPLE AND BLACKBERRY CRUMBLE

This is my favourite crumble as I love the texture and taste of cooked apple, and the late-summer flavour of blackberries makes it extra special. But you can use anything you like for this crumble, with different mixes of fruit and varying amounts of sugar depending on the sweetness of the fruit. I don't like my crumbles to be too sweet, so I add only a little sugar to the apples and blackberries.

Serves 6
8 apples, half-peeled, alternating stripes of
   peel and flesh, cored and sliced, plus 1 extra
   apple if needed
250 g (2¼ cups) blackberries
2 tablespoons caster (superfine) sugar
pinch of ground cinnamon
double (heavy) cream or Crème Anglaise
   (see page 42), to serve

For the topping
200 g (1⅓ cups) plain (all-purpose) flour or
220 g (1⅓ cups) wholemeal (wholewheat) flour
120 g (generous ½ cup) cold unsalted butter
100 g (½ cup) light brown or demerara sugar
pinch of salt

Preheat the oven to 190°C/375°F/Gas Mark 5.

Put the apples in a bowl and add the blackberries, caster sugar and cinnamon. Mix lightly and put in a 25 x 20 cm (10 x 8 inch) baking dish. If the mixture looks too flat, half-peel and slice another apple and add it. The mixture must be raised as the fruit shrinks a lot.

Now make the topping. If you are using a food processor, process the flour, butter, brown sugar and salt until until the mixture has a light, crumbly texture. Otherwise, cut the butter into small pieces, mix the dry ingredients together and rub the butter into them with your fingers.

Sprinkle the mixture over the apples and blackberries and bake for 40–50 minutes till the topping is golden and crisp and the fruit is tender.

Serve hot with cream or crème anglaise.

A NEW DELIVERY FROM THE
'MADE IN CLEY' COOPERATIVE

OAT AND APPLE BETTY

Bettys are traditionally made with breadcrumbs (see Apple Brown Betty, right), but this one is a cross between a crumble and a Betty.

Serves 6
60 g (¼ cup) **unsalted butter, plus extra for greasing**
4 large cooking apples or 8 medium apples, peeled, cored and sliced
grated zest and juice of 2 lemons
2 tablespoons marmalade
double (heavy) **cream or Crème Anglaise (see page 42), to serve**

For the topping
120 g (generous ¾ cup) **plain** (all-purpose) **flour**
120 g (scant 1⅔ cups) **rolled oats**
120 g (generous ½ cup) **cold unsalted butter**
pinch of ground cinnamon
pinch of salt
120 g (generous ½ cup) **demerara sugar**

Preheat the oven to 190°C/375°F/Gas Mark 5 and butter a 25 x 20 cm (10 x 8 inch) **baking dish.**

Put the apples in a bowl and add the lemon zest and juice and the marmalade. Mix well together and set aside.

Now make the topping. If you are using a food processor, process the flour, oats, butter, cinnamon, salt and sugar until the mixture has a light, crumbly texture. Otherwise, cut the butter into small pieces, mix the dry ingredients together and rub the butter into them with your fingers.

Put half the apple mixture into the prepared baking dish and sprinkle with half the oat-and-flour mixture. Spread this with the remaining apples and top with the remaining oats and flour.

Dot with the butter and bake for about 45 minutes till the topping is golden and the apples are tender.

Serve warm with cream or crème anglaise.

APPLE BROWN BETTY

Brown Bettys can also be made from fruits like rhubarb, plums and blackberries but I think apples are the best.

Serves 6–8
2 tablespoons unsalted butter, plus extra for greasing
1.5 kg (3 pounds 3 ounces) **cooking apples (ideally Bramleys), peeled, cored and thinly sliced**
100 g (½ cup) **caster** (superfine) **sugar**
grated zest and juice of 1 lemon
crème fraîche (or thick sour cream)**, to serve**

For the breadcrumbs
60 g (¼ cup) **unsalted butter**
160 g (generous 1½ cups) **fresh breadcrumbs**
60 g (⅓ cup) **light brown sugar**
1 teaspoon ground cinnamon
1 teaspoon ground mixed spice

Preheat the oven to 180°C/350°F/Gas Mark 4 and butter a 25 x 20 cm (10 x 8 inch) **baking dish.**

To prepare the breadcrumbs, put the butter in a saucepan and melt over a low heat. Add the breadcrumbs and stir over a medium heat until they are crisp and light golden. Remove from the heat and add the sugar, cinnamon and mixed spice. Set aside to cool.

Meanwhile, put the apples in a bowl with the sugar and lemon zest and juice, and mix well.

Put one-third of the breadcrumbs on the base of the prepared baking dish.

Spread half the apples over them, and sprinkle with another one-third of the breadcrumbs.

Add the remaining apples and top these with the last of the breadcrumbs. Dot with the butter and bake for about 45 minutes until the breadcrumbs are golden and the apples are tender.

Serve warm with crème fraîche.

LUIS, ON A THURSDAY AFTERNOON

RICE PUDDING/RIZ AU LAIT

You either love or loathe this – the emotions that are produced at the mention of this simplest of puddings are amazing. My mother and I could eat a whole one by ourselves while the rest of the family look on with total lack of interest!

Serves 6–8
100 g (½ cup) **round rice, washed and drained** (We use an Italian round rice called 'tonde ballila' at the bakery)
1 litre (4 cups) **full-cream milk, heated to just under boiling point**
1 vanilla pod (bean)
1 tablespoon unsalted butter
2 tablespoons caster (superfine) **sugar, to taste** (It's all a question of taste!)
50 ml (¼ cup) **single** (light) **cream**
pinch of grated nutmeg
single (light) **cream, honey or light brown sugar, to serve**

Preheat the oven to **140°C/275°F/Gas Mark 1.**

Place the rice in a baking dish, big enough to take **1.5 litres** (6 cups) of liquid, with just over half the heated milk, and the vanilla pod, butter and caster sugar.

Bake for about 3 hours. After 1 hour, stir the rice and add more hot milk to keep it moist, but not drowned.

After about 2 hours, add the remaining milk (hot is better, but not necessary) and the cream and remove the vanilla pod. Sprinkle with the nutmeg.

Continue baking till the top is light golden and the rice has a thick, creamy consistency. It must never dry out to a stodgy mass.

Serve warm with extra cream, honey or simply brown sugar.

TOFFEE PUDDINGS

A very popular dessert which we serve only in winter. Our customers are completely baffled as to what it's made from – so here's what's in it and how to make it.

Serves 8
220 g (1¼ cups) **dried apricots, very finely chopped**
1 teaspoon bicarbonate of soda (baking soda)
215 g (generous 1 cup) **dark brown sugar**
205 g (scant 1 cup) **unsalted butter, softened**
8 tablespoons single (light) **cream**
100 g (½ cup) **caster** (superfine) **sugar**
1 teaspoon natural vanilla extract
1 egg
225 g (1½ cups) **plain** (all-purpose) **flour, sifted**
1 teaspoon baking powder
pinch of salt
Crème Anglaise (see page 42), **to serve**

Place the apricots in a bowl, pour **300 ml** (1¼ cups) boiling water over them and add the bicarbonate of soda. Set aside until cool.

Put the dark brown sugar, **115 g** (½ cup) of the butter and the cream in a saucepan and cook over a low heat, stirring, until the mixture is smooth and the sugar has melted. Do not let it bubble and boil as it may separate.

Pour into eight ramekins (about 3 tablespoons in each) and leave to cool.

Preheat the oven to **180°C/350°F/Gas Mark 4.**

Beat the remaining butter with the caster sugar and vanilla extract until light. Add the egg and beat well.

Fold in the flour, baking powder and salt.

Finally, fold in the cooled apricots.

Mix well and divide between the ramekins. Don't overfill them – they should be about three-quarters full.

Put the ramekins in a bain marie with enough water to come one-third of the way up their sides, and cover with foil.

Bake for about 30 minutes until just set.

Turn the puddings out on to individual plates and serve warm with crème anglaise.

TOFFEE PUDDINGS

RICE, COCONUT AND TROPICAL FRUIT CAKES

We make these cakes in ramekins. They are especially good when mangoes or pineapples are in season and the fruit is at its sweetest!

Serves 8
60 g (¼ cup) **unsalted butter, softened,** plus extra for greasing
150 g (scant ⅔ cup) **round or risotto rice,** washed and drained
400 ml (1¾ cups) **coconut milk**
300 ml (1¼ cups) **single** (light) **cream**
pinch of salt
3 eggs, beaten
90 g (scant ½ cup) **caster** (superfine) **sugar**
½ teaspoon natural vanilla extract
grated zest of 1 lime
1 mango or ½ pineapple, peeled and finely sliced

Preheat the oven to 180°C / 350°F / Gas Mark 4.

Butter eight ramekins and line them with parchment paper.

Put the rice, coconut milk and cream in a saucepan with the salt and bring slowly to the boil. Turn the heat down to a simmer and cook till most of the liquid has gone and the rice is soft – about 45 minutes.

Remove from the heat, and beat in the eggs, sugar, butter, vanilla extract and lime zest.

Pour into the prepared ramekins and place a mango or pineapple slice on top of each serving.

Bake for about 25 minutes until just set. Cool for a while before turning out.

Serve warm or chilled.

OUR CLASSIC CHOCOLATE MOUSSE

Serves 6–8
200 g (7 ounces) **roughly chopped dark** (bittersweet) **chocolate (at least 70% cocoa solids)**
4 eggs, separated
200 ml (scant 1 cup) **double** (heavy) **cream**
1 tablespoon caster (superfine) **sugar**
whipped cream, and chocolate shavings (optional), to serve

Put the chocolate in a heatproof bowl with 2 tablespoons water, place the bowl over a saucepan of simmering water and cook over a low heat until the chocolate has melted and is smooth and shiny.

Remove from the heat, add the egg yolks and beat well.

In another bowl, whip the cream until it forms soft peaks and fold it into the chocolate.

In a third bowl, beat the egg whites until they form soft peaks, then quickly beat in the sugar.

Fold the egg whites carefully into the chocolate, half the quantity at a time – the first addition will loosen the chocolate, the second will make it light.

Pour into a bowl or individual glasses and chill in the fridge for about 1 hour.

Serve with extra whipped cream and perhaps some chocolate shavings.

OUR CLASSIC CHOCOLATE MOUSSE

CARAMEL ICE CREAM

A delicious, intense, and not too sweet,
ice cream.

Serves 8–10
550 g (2¾ cups) **caster** (superfine) **sugar**
1 litre (4 cups) **milk**
1 litre (4 cups) **single** (light) **cream**
14 egg yolks
pinch of salt

Put the sugar and **120 ml** (½ cup) **water** in a
saucepan big enough to take all the milk and
cream. Heat gently at first till the sugar has
dissolved, then turn the heat to high and cook
until the syrup is golden amber – a deep caramel
colour. Don't stir. Just shake the pan to get an
even colour. And keep a constant eye on it as
caramel must never be left alone!

Meanwhile, heat the milk and cream in another
saucepan till scalded.

In a bowl, beat the egg yolks with the salt
(If you prefer, you can heat the milk and cream
and beat the eggs before you start the caramel).

When the caramel has reached the right colour,
immediately remove it from the heat and place
the saucepan in the sink in case of spills.

Gently and slowly pour in a little of the hot
cream, taking great care as it may bubble
up furiously over the saucepan.

When things have calmed down add the rest
of the cream, whisking continuously till all
the cream is in the caramel.

Slowly whisk the beaten egg yolks into the
slightly cooled cream.

Strain and refrigerate till cold.

Pour into an ice-cream maker and freeze
according to the manufacturer's instructions.

SUMMER PUDDING

Serves 8
1 loaf of good-quality white bread or brioche,
  thinly sliced and crusts removed
250 g (1¼ cups) **caster** (superfine) **sugar**
250 g (2¼ cups) **strawberries, hulled and sliced**
500 g (4½ cups) **raspberries**
500 g (4½ cups) **blackberries**
250 g (2¼ cups) **blueberries**
250 g (2¼ cups) **red currants, stripped from**
  their stems
whipped cream, to serve

Line the base and sides of a **25 cm** (10 inch)
pudding basin with slices of bread or brioche,
keeping back some slices for the lid and
middle layer. Make sure there are no gaps
between the slices. Set aside.

Put the sugar and **200 ml** (scant 1 cup) **water** in
a large saucepan and bring to the boil over a
gentle heat, stirring constantly until the sugar
has dissolved.

Add all the fruit and cook over a very low
heat for a few minutes – just long enough for
the syrup to be coloured by the fruit – then
remove the pan from the heat. The fruit
should be half-mashed and half-whole, giving
off lots of juice.

Reserve 2–3 tablespoons of the juice to use to
soak the bread if necessary and put half the
fruit into the pudding basin.

Add a layer of bread or brioche slices, then
pour in the remaining fruit and cover with a
'lid' of bread or brioche. Make sure the lid is
soaked with juice. If it seems a bit dry, add
some of the reserved juice.

Press down well and cover with a plate that
fits inside the basin. Place a weight on top
and refrigerate overnight.

Unmould on to a serving plate and top with
whipped cream.

A PRESENT FROM NOA

ETON MESS

I can only guess at the origins of this simple but very popular dessert. We used to make pavlovas, but Eton Mess seems to have replaced them and the abundance of red fruits in Paris in June just begs for it to be made. It is so simple. You will need homemade meringues, whipped cream and lots of red fruits. In winter we often do a 'Winter Eton Mess' with meringues, whipped cream, chestnut purée and chocolate sauce!

Serves 8
unsalted butter, for greasing
4 egg whites
200 g (1 cup) **caster** (superfine) **sugar, plus 1 tablespoon**
dash of natural vanilla extract
500 ml (2 cups) **double** (heavy) **cream**
300 g (scant 3 cups) **strawberries, hulled**

Preheat the oven to 120°C / 250°F / Gas Mark ½.

Butter a baking tray and line it with parchment paper.

To make the meringues, beat the egg whites in a bowl until firm and white. Gradually whisk in **200 g** (1 cup) sugar and finally add the vanilla extract.

Put giant spoonfuls on the prepared baking tray and bake till the meringues are almost dry, but still a bit gooey in the middle – about 3 hours. Set aside to cool.

In another bowl, whip the cream till it forms soft peaks.

Put a quarter of the strawberries in a food processor with 1 tablespoon sugar and process to make a purée, or put them through a sieve and mix in the sugar. Set aside.

Cut the remaining strawberries into pieces and roughly break the cooled meringues by hand.

Now all you have to do is gently fold together the crushed meringues, whipped cream and strawberries in a ratio that pleases you (more fruit, more meringues or more cream).

Pour the puréed strawberries on top and serve immediately, or chill in the fridge till needed.

eton mess
* avec creme *
3.50 €

ETON MESS

APRICOT SORBET

I just have to include a sorbet made with
my favourite fruit.

Serves 6–8
1.2 kg (2½ pounds) **apricots, halved and stoned**
200 g (1 cup) **caster** (superfine) **sugar**
juice of 1 lemon (optional)

Put the apricots in a saucepan with **50 ml** (¼ cup)
water and cook over a very low heat until they
are soft – about 20 minutes. Transfer them to a
food processor and process to make a purée, or
put them through a sieve. Strain and set aside.

Put the sugar and **250 ml** (1 cup) **water** in
another saucepan and bring to the boil over a
gentle heat, stirring constantly until the sugar
has dissolved.

Remove from the heat and set aside to cool.

Add the apricot purée to the syrup. If the
mixture is too sweet add the lemon juice.

Refrigerate till cold, then pour into an
ice-cream maker and freeze according to the
manufacturer's instructions.

RED BEAN SORBET

I love the red bean sweets and desserts you
find in Japan. They have a texture very similar
to that of our chestnut purée.

Serves 6–8
250 g (generous 1¼ cups) **adzuki beans, soaked**
overnight in 3 times their volume of water
220 g (1 cup) **caster** (superfine) **sugar**
1 teaspoon natural vanilla extract

Drain the beans, put them in a saucepan with
double their volume of fresh water and bring
to the boil.

Drain them again, put them back in the
saucepan with the same amount of fresh water,
then turn the heat down and simmer the beans
for about 2 hours. Keep adding water if they
start to dry out and skim the surface carefully.
When the beans are completely soft, drain
them and put them in a bowl.

Meanwhile, put the sugar and **250 ml** (1 cup)
water in another saucepan and bring to the boil
over a gentle heat, stirring constantly until the
sugar has dissolved.

Add the vanilla extract.

Cool slightly and add to the beans.

Put the mixture in a food processor and process
to make a purée, or put it through a sieve.
Strain and refrigerate till cold.

Pour into an ice-cream maker and freeze
according to the manufacturer's instructions.

THE END OF THE DAY

INDEX

ACKNOWLEDGEMENTS

Without a doubt, if Richard & Amanda had not walked
into Rose Bakery and suggested a cookbook, I might never
have dared. I thank them, Alex and all the staff at Phaidon
for their hard work and understanding. An enormous thank
you to Nikki, Catherine and Adrian who had faith and
generosity. To Toby Glanville for his beautiful photography,
humour and kindness. To Frith, Marianne and Amelia for
designing this beautiful book, and to James Graham for
drawing the map. To Rei, for the little jewel on the 4th floor
of Dover Street Market. A grateful «merci» to Lindy for her
painted wall and recommending the 9th arrondissement
in the first place, and to Alice who helped us open Rose
Bakery as my assistant chef with such enthusiasm. Finally,
thank you to all our customers who keep coming back,
and who inspire and encourage us to continue. Finally
to my mother Mary, a thank you for feeding me so well
as I was growing up, and for therefore obviously being
my first inspiration.

This is for Kim and Marissa, who have been through
everything with us, with love.

CERNAM, KERRY, MIRANDA, WONDY, SARA JANE, ROSE,
JEAN-CHARLES, DAVID, KAORI, JOEL, SEAN AND FEDERICA

ROSE & JEAN-CHARLES CARRARINI

MERCI
&
THANKYOU

LINDY'S PAINTING

Phaidon Press Limited
Regent's Wharf
All Saints Street
London N1 9PA

Phaidon Press Inc.
180 Varick Street
New York, NY 10014

First published 2006
Reprinted 2008, 2009, 2010 (twice), 2011
© 2006 Phaidon Press Limited

ISBN 978 0 7148 4465 7

A CIP catalogue record for this book
is available from the British Library.

Photographs by Toby Glanville
Designed by Kerr|Noble

Printed in China

www.phaidon.com

FIN

FERMÉ

19 HEURES